The Power Threat Meaning
Framework: Overview

January 2018

This publication has been produced by the British Psychological Society's Division of Clinical Psychology as a Member Network publication and represents the views and expert contributions of its authors.

Citation

In text: Johnstone, L. & Boyle, M. (2018)
In bibliographies and any list of publications: Johnstone, L. & Boyle, M. with Cromby, J., Dillon, J., Harper, D., Kinderman, P., Longden, E., Pilgrim, D. & Read, J. (2018). *The Power Threat Meaning Framework: Overview.* Leicester: British Psychological Society.

A catalogue record for this book is available from the British Library.

ISBN 978-1-85433-756-6

Published by
The British Psychological Society
St Andrews House
48 Princess Road East
Leicester LE1 7DR
www.bps.org.uk

If you have problems reading this document and would like it in a different format, please contact us with your specific requirements.

Tel: 0116 252 9523; Email: P4P@bps.org.uk.

Contents

Acknowledgements

Lead authors

- **Dr Lucy Johnstone,** Consultant Clinical Psychologist and Independent Trainer
- **Professor Mary Boyle,** Professor Emeritus of Clinical Psychology, University of East London

Contributing authors/project group

- **Dr John Cromby,** Reader in Psychology, ULSB, University of Leicester
- **Dr Jacqui Dillon,** Survivor Activist and National Chair, Hearing Voices Network, England
- **Dr David Harper,** Reader in Clinical Psychology, University of East London
- **Dr Eleanor Longden,** Postdoctoral Service User Research Manager, Psychosis Research Unit, Greater Manchester Mental Health NHS Foundation Trust
- **Professor Peter Kinderman,** Professor of Clinical Psychology, University of Liverpool
- **Professor David Pilgrim,** Honorary Professor of Health and Social Policy, University of Liverpool
- **Professor John Read,** Professor of Clinical Psychology, University of East London

Research and editorial assistance

- **Dr Kate Allsopp,** Research Associate, University of Liverpool

Service user/carer consultancy group

- **Lucy Goldsmith**
- **Nicky Hayward**
- **Sam Shakes**
- Five others who wish to remain anonymous

Critical reader group

With a particular remit to address diversity issues:

- **Jan Bostock,** Consultant Clinical Psychologist and Professional Lead, Northumberland Tyne & Wear NHS Foundation Trust
- **Dr Jonathan Gadsby,** Research Fellow, Mental Health and Learning Disabilities Nursing, Birmingham City University
- **Dr Sarah Kamens,** Postdoctoral Fellow in Psychology, Wesleyan University, USA;
- **Guilaine Kinouani,** Psychotherapist & Equality Consultant
- **Gilli Watson,** Consultant Clinical Psychologist, Devon Partnership NHS Trust.

Additional contributions

- **Dr Kate Allsopp,** Research Associate, University of Liverpool
- **Alison Branitsky,** Mount Holyoke College, USA
- **Dr Maria Castro Romero,** Senior Lecturer in Clinical Psychology, University of East London, for assistance with interviewing and with Chapter 7 of the main publication
- **Dr Samantha Cole,** Consultant Clinical Psychologist (Health Psychology)
- **Dr Selma Ebrahim,** Consultant Clinical Psychologist
- **Dr Jo Ramsden,** Consultant Clinical Psychologist (Forensic Services)
- **Dr Clive Weston,** Consultant Clinical Psychologist (Intellectual Disability)
- **Phil Wilshire,** Professional Head of Social Care and Social Work, Avon and Wiltshire Mental Health Partnership NHS Trust, for significant input into Chapter 8 of the main publication.

Appendices

Thanks to:

- **Ishtiaq Ahmed,** Community Development Manager, Sharing Voices Bradford
- **Isabel Clarke,** Consultant Clinical Psychologist
- **Dr Angela Kennedy,** Consultant Clinical Psychologist
- **Dr Shelley McCann,** Clinical Psychologist
- **Professor Nimisha Patel,** Professor of Clinical Psychology
- **Dr Sami Timimi,** Consultant Child and Adolescent Psychiatrist
- **Fiona Venner,** Chief Executive of Leeds Survivor Led Crisis Service
- Members of MAC-UK.

Reviewers

We are grateful for comments on the final published version from representatives of the DCP executive, the DCP 'Beyond diagnosis' Committee, and the Psychosis and Complex Mental Health Faculty.

Thanks are also due the following for their help and support with the project:

- **Dr Steven Coles,** former chair of the 'Beyond diagnosis' group
- **Richard Pemberton,** former DCP Chair
- **Dr Esther Cohen-Tovée,** DCP Chair
- **Helen Barnett,** Division Advisor, Member Network Services
- **Dr Stephen Weatherhead,** former Director, DCP Professional Standards Unit.

Introduction

In 2013, the Division of Clinical Psychology of the British Psychological Society published a Position Statement entitled *Classification of behaviour and experience in relation to functional psychiatric diagnoses: Time for a paradigm shift*. It was issued in the context of widespread acknowledgement that current classification systems such as DSM and ICD are fundamentally flawed. Recommendation 3 of the position paper is: 'To support work, in conjunction with service users, on developing a multi-factorial and contextual approach, which incorporates social, psychological and biological factors' (p.9). The framework described here, the Power Threat Meaning Framework, is the result of a project for work towards fulfilling this aim.

The project team's aim was to produce a foundational document which sets out the philosophical, theoretical and empirical basis for such a framework and describes how it can serve as a conceptual alternative to psychiatric classification in relation to emotional distress and troubled or troubling behaviour. There are, and have always been, alternatives to diagnosis on an individual, one-to-one basis, such as problem descriptions and formulations. What we have so far lacked is a supporting conceptual framework which works at a broader clustering and pattern-identification level.

The Power Threat Meaning Framework has the potential to take us beyond medicalisation and diagnostic assumptions. It puts forward alternative ways of thinking about a range of fundamental issues including: What kinds of theoretical frameworks and assumptions are appropriate for understanding emotional distress, unusual experiences and troubled and troubling behaviour? What research methods could be used and what counts as evidence? How could the results of research be interpreted? What is the relationship between personal distress and its wider social, material and cultural contexts? How can we centre people's lived experiences and the meanings that shape them? What new conceptualisations arise from all these questions, and how can all the implications be translated into practice, both within and beyond services, at all levels from individual to social policy?

It is essential to recognise that there is a range of patient/service user/survivor/carer perspectives on psychiatric diagnosis. The project team includes survivors as well as professionals, and these views and experiences are central to the arguments (Chapter 7 of the main publication describes the consultation process with service users/carers). Whatever people's personal views, in the short and medium term psychiatric diagnoses will still be required for access to services, benefits and so on. Equally, we all have a right to describe our experiences in the way that makes most sense to us. In the longer term, this Framework is intended to support the construction of non-diagnostic, non-blaming, de-mystifying stories about strength and survival, which re-integrate many behaviours and reactions currently diagnosed as symptoms of mental disorder back into the range of universal human experience.

The project documents

The project outcomes are presented in two forms: a longer, more detailed version, known as the *main publication** (available from: www.bps.org.uk/PTM-Main); and this shorter document, known as the *overview publication* (available from: www.bps.org.uk/PTM-Overview). This overview publication is also available in printed format; please email MemberNetworkServices@bps.org.uk to request a copy. Each version will now be described.

The main publication

The main publication is entitled: *The Power Threat Meaning Framework: Towards the identification of patterns in emotional distress, unusual experiences and troubled or troubling behaviour, as an alternative to functional psychiatric diagnosis.*

It supplements the overview publication by:

- setting out the problems of medicalisation and psychiatric diagnosis, why these problems have arisen and why they cannot be resolved without fundamental shifts in thinking;
- showing the relationship between the aims of diagnosis in medicine and psychiatry, and the aims of this alternative framework;
- offering a detailed account of the underlying philosophical principles, theories and evidence supporting the Power Threat Meaning (PTM) Framework;
- reporting on the views of the consultancy group of service users and carers who gave feedback on the PTM Framework as it developed;
- discussing the practical implications of adopting a non-diagnostic approach in the areas of service commissioning, design and delivery, therapeutic practice, research, legal practice, access to welfare and other benefits, and in relation to society as a whole in terms of social policy, equality and social justice;
- supplying full references for all the above;
- supplying indicative references for the General Patterns and sub-patterns derived from the PTM Framework.

Readers wanting an in-depth understanding of the context, principles, research and practice from which the PTM Framework emerged, may wish to read the main publication in its entirety. Alternatively, or additionally, it may be useful to refer to specific chapters in order to supply more detail about particular aspects of the PTM Framework.

The content of the main publication is:

- Executive Summary
- Introduction
- Chapter 1: Problems of medicalisation and diagnosis
- Chapter 2: Conceptual and philosophical issues
- Chapter 3: Meaning and narrative
- Chapter 4: The social context

---

* Johnstone, L. & Boyle, M. with Cromby, J., Dillon, J., Harper, D., Kinderman, P., Longden, E., Pilgrim, D. & Read, J. (2018). *The Power Threat Meaning Framework: Towards the identification of patterns in emotional distress, unusual experiences and troubled or troubling behaviour, as an alternative to functional psychiatric diagnosis.* Leicester: British Psychological Society. Available from: www.bps.org.uk/PTM-Main

- Chapter 5: The role of biology
- Chapter 6: The Power Threat Meaning Framework
- Chapter 7: Service user consultation
- Chapter 8: Ways forward
- Appendix 1: Evidence supporting the General Patterns

The overview publication

The shorter overview publication is entitled: *The Power Threat Meaning Framework: Overview.*

This version stands on its own, although as above, readers may wish to refer to the main publication for more detail about particular aspects. This printed version offers a brief summary of the principles and evidence from which the PTM Framework emerged, but its main focus is on the PTM Framework itself and the General Patterns derived from it. It thus approximates to Chapter 6 of the longer document. In addition, it includes appendices illustrating some of the ways in which non-diagnostic practice has already been successfully adopted both within and beyond services.

This overview publication is structured as follows:

- **Part 1:** Summary of the PTM Framework, its core principles, purposes and scope. This brief summary orients the reader to the main features of the PTM Framework.
- **Part 2:** Summary of theory and research underpinning the PTM Framework. This briefly recaps some of the conclusions from the literature on the role of factors from various fields, including biological, psychological, social, political and cultural, in the origins and persistence of emotional distress and troubling behaviour.
- **Part 3:** The Power Threat Meaning Framework. This demonstrates how theory and research can be used to support a meta-approach, the Power Threat Meaning Framework. The relationship between the various elements of the PTM Framework is illustrated through the Foundational Power Threat Meaning Pattern.
- **Part 4:** Provisional General Patterns arising out of the Foundational Pattern. Some General Patterns that emerge from the Foundational Power Threat Meaning Pattern are outlined. These patterns can be used as a basis and resource for the co-construction of new personal and social narratives, as well as suggesting alternatives to diagnosis for service delivery/administrative/legal/service planning/research and related purposes.
- **Part 5:** Personal narratives within the Power Threat Meaning Framework. The role, purpose and possible formats of personal narratives within the PTM Framework are illustrated and discussed, along with options for non-medical language use.

Both the longer and shorter documents are envisaged as the outcomes of the first stage of a larger ongoing project. Much further work will be needed in order to translate their principles into action. One of the primary aims of this work will be to produce or co-produce materials for diverse audiences including service users/survivors, carers, students and trainees, professionals, researchers, commissioners, policy makers and the general public.

Reference

Division of Clinical Psychology (2013). *Classification of behaviour and experience in relation to functional psychiatric diagnosis: Time for a paradigm shift.* Leicester: British Psychological Society.

Part 1: An outline of the Framework, its core principles, purpose and scope

The Power Threat Meaning (PTM) Framework is a meta framework. It draws upon a variety of models, practices and philosophical traditions but is broader than and not reliant on any particular theoretical orientation. Rather, the aim is to inform and expand existing approaches by offering a fundamentally different perspective on the origins, experience and expression of emotional distress and troubled or troubling behaviour.

The PTM Framework is based on the following core principles:

- Constructive alternatives to psychiatric classification and diagnosis need to focus on aspects of human functioning which have been marginalised in theoretical frameworks derived from the study of bodily processes or objects in the physical world. In particular, alternatives should be based on the study of embodied humans behaving purposefully in social and relational contexts.

- 'Abnormal' behaviour and experience exist on a continuum with 'normal' behaviour and experience and are subject to similar frameworks of understanding and interpretation. These include the assumption that, unless there is strong evidence to the contrary, our behaviour and experience can be seen as intelligible responses to our current circumstances, history, belief systems, culture, and bodily capacities, although the links amongst these may not always be obvious or straightforward.

- Causality in human distress and behaviour is probabilistic; that is, it has an 'on average' character and it will never be possible to predict precise impacts. Causal influences also operate contingently and synergistically, meaning that the effects of any one factor are always mediated by and contingent upon others, and that influences can magnify each others' effects.

- Experiences and expressions of emotional distress are enabled and mediated by, but not in any simplistic sense caused by, our bodies and biology.

- Humans are fundamentally social beings whose experiences of distress and troubled or troubling behaviour are inseparable from their material, social, environmental, socio-economic, and cultural contexts. There is no separate 'disorder' to be explained, with context as an additional influence.

- All indigenous forms of understanding distress have useful aspects, but there can be no 'global Psychiatry' or 'global Psychology'. Patterns in emotional and behavioural difficulties will always reflect prevailing social and cultural discourses, norms and expectations, including accepted conceptualisations of personhood.

- Theories and judgements about identifying, explaining and intervening in mental distress and troubling behaviour are not interest- or value-free. This does not mean that useful and reliable knowledge is unobtainable but that trying to separate 'facts' from values is highly problematic.

- We need to take meaning, narrative and subjective experience seriously. This will involve a central place for the narratives of experts by experience. It will also involve drawing on a wide range of research methods and giving equivalent status to qualitative and quantitative methods, including the testimony of service users/survivors and carers themselves.

These principles inform the PTM Framework's main features and purposes, which are as follows:

- It allows provisional identification of general patterns and regularities in the expression and experience of distress and troubled or troubling behaviour, as opposed to specific biological or psychological causal mechanisms linked to discrete disorder categories.
- It shows how these response patterns are evident to varying degrees and in varying circumstances for all individuals across the lifespan.
- It does not assume 'pathology'; rather, it describes coping and survival mechanisms which may be more or less functional as an adaptation to particular conflicts and adversities in both the past and present.
- It integrates the influence of biological/genetic and epigenetic/evolutionary factors in mediating and enabling these response patterns.
- It integrates relational, social, cultural and material factors as shaping the emergence, persistence, experience and expression of these patterns.
- It accounts for cultural differences in the experience and expression of distress.
- It assigns a central role to personal meaning, emerging out of social and cultural discourses and belief systems, material conditions and bodily potentialities.
- It assigns a central role to personal agency, or the ability to exercise influence within inevitable psychosocial, biological and material constraints.
- It acknowledges the centrality of the relational/social/political context in decisions about what counts as a 'mental health' need or crisis in any given situation.
- It provides an evidence base for drawing on general patterns of coping and survival responses to inform individual/family/group narratives.
- It offers alternative ways of fulfilling the service-related, administrative and research functions of diagnosis.
- It suggests alternative language uses, while arguing that there can be no one-to-one replacements for current diagnostic terms.
- It includes meanings and implications for action in a wider community/social policy/ political context.

An outline of the PTM Framework

This broad PTM Framework is derived from a wide range of theory and research, across disciplines and research methods. It comprises four interrelated aspects:

1. The operation of **POWER** (biological/embodied; coercive; legal; economic/material; ideological; social/cultural; and interpersonal).
2. The **THREAT** that the negative operation of power may pose to the person, the group and the community, with particular reference to emotional distress, and the ways in which this is mediated by our biology.
3. The central role of **MEANING** (as produced within social and cultural discourses, and primed by evolved and acquired bodily responses) in shaping the operation, experience and expression of power, threat, and our responses to threat.
4. As a reaction to all the above, the learned and evolved **THREAT RESPONSES** that a person, or family, group or community, may need to draw upon in order to ensure emotional, physical, relational and social survival. These range from largely automatic physiological reactions to linguistically-based or consciously selected actions and responses.

Unlike the more traditional biopsychosocial model of mental distress, there is no assumption of pathology and the 'biological' aspects are not privileged, but constitute one level of explanation, inextricably linked to all the others. Equally important, although a tripartite model is a convenient heuristic, the four elements of Power, Threat, Meaning and Threat Response are not independent, but evolve out of each other. The individual does not exist, and cannot be understood, separately from his/her relationships, community and culture; meaning only arises when social, cultural and biological elements combine; and biological capacities cannot be separated from the social and interpersonal environment. Within this, 'meaning' is intrinsic to the expression and experience of all forms of emotional distress, giving unique shape to the individual's personal responses.

In summary, this PTM Framework for the origins and maintenance of distress replaces the question at the heart of medicalisation, 'What is wrong with you?' with four others:

- 'What has happened to you?' (How has **Power** operated in your life?)
- 'How did it affect you?' (What kind of **Threats** does this pose?)
- 'What sense did you make of it?' (What is the **Meaning** of these situations and experiences to you?)
- 'What did you have to do to survive?' (What kinds of **Threat Response** are you using?)

Translated into practice with an individual, family or group, two additional questions need to be asked:

- 'What are your strengths?' (What access to **Power resources** do you have?)
- ...and to integrate all the above: 'What is your story?'

A key purpose of the PTM Framework is to aid the provisional identification of evidence-based patterns in distress, unusual experiences and troubled or troubling behaviour. In contrast to the specific biological causal mechanisms which support some medical disorder categories, these patterns are highly probabilistic, with influences operating contingently and synergistically. However, this does not mean that no regularities exist. Rather, it implies that these regularities are not, as in medicine, fundamentally patterns in biology, but *patterns of embodied, meaning-based threat responses to the negative operation of power.*

The PTM Framework demonstrates how these probabilistic patterns can be described at various levels, starting with the 'Foundational Pattern in the Power Threat Meaning Framework'. This sets the scene for the identification of seven Provisional General Patterns which emerge from within the Foundational Pattern. They are not one-to-one replacements for diagnostic clusters, but are based on broad regularities which cut across diagnostic groups, and which arise out of personal, social and cultural meanings.

Each Provisional General Pattern includes a range of possible Threat Responses grouped in terms of the functions they are serving. Conversely, each type of Threat Response may appear within several different General Patterns, and may serve a range of different functions.

These Provisional General Patterns fulfil one of the main aims of the Framework, which is to restore the links between meaning-based threats and meaning-based threat responses. These responses arise out of core human needs to be protected, valued, find a place in the social group, and so on, and represent people's attempts, conscious and otherwise, to survive the negative impacts of power. Understood as 'survival strategies' rather than 'symptoms', they cut across diagnoses, across specialties, and across the boundaries of what is usually considered 'normal' versus 'pathological.' They are present at some points and to some degree in everyone's daily life.

The PTM Framework and the patterns derived from it also provide a new perspective on the application of Western psychiatric classification systems to non-Western cultures and expressions of distress, both within the UK and around the world. The PTM Framework predicts and allows for the existence of widely varying cultural experiences and expressions of distress without positioning them as bizarre, primitive, less valid, or as exotic variations of the dominant diagnostic paradigm. Since patterns in emotional distress will always be to an extent local to time and place, there can never be a universal lexicon of such patterns. However, viewed as a meta-framework that is based on universal evolved human capabilities and threat responses, the core principles of the PTM Framework apply across time and across cultures. Within this, open-ended lists of threat responses and functions allow for an indefinite number of locally and historically specific expressions of distress, all shaped by prevailing cultural meanings.

More specifically, the PTM Framework can suggest alternatives to diagnosis for clustering/ administrative/legal/service planning/research purposes. It can inform the construction, or co-construction, of personal narratives and open up the possibility for different, non-diagnostic stories of strength and survival. Along with this, it offers a way of more effectively fulfilling some of the reported benefits of diagnosis, such as providing an explanation, having distress validated, facilitating contact with others in similar circumstances, offering relief from shame and guilt, suggesting a way forward and conveying hope for positive change.

Scope of the PTM Framework

The General Patterns derived from the PTM Framework encompass what is sometimes called 'functional psychiatric diagnoses', i.e. groupings of thoughts, feelings and behaviours for which no organic cause has been identified. The PTM Framework is also relevant to problematic forms of behaviour including some of those seen in the fields of addictions and criminal justice. Although the core principles of the PTM Framework apply across cultures, the main focus of the project is on countries that have adopted or are in the process of adopting standard psychiatric classification systems such as *DSM* and *ICD*. The Global Mental Health Movement means that this is an expanding territory. (This and related issues are discussed in detail in Chapters 2 and 3 of the main publication.*)

The PTM Framework is not intended to apply to the direct effects of conditions like dementia, intellectual disabilities, neurological or neurodegenerative disorders and the consequences of stroke, brain injury, infections in older adults, and so on. Problems arising from the immediate effects of street drugs are also excluded. Autism has not been considered as a specific diagnosis; instead, readers are referred to the excellent debates about this complex topic at the Exeter University 'Exploring Diagnosis' project (http://blogs.exeter.ac.uk/exploringdiagnosis/).

---

* Johnstone, L. & Boyle, M. with Cromby, J., Dillon, J., Harper, D., Kinderman, P., Longden, E., Pilgrim, D. & Read, J. (2018). *The Power Threat Meaning Framework: Towards the identification of patterns in emotional distress, unusual experiences and troubled or troubling behaviour, as an alternative to functional psychiatric diagnosis.* Leicester: British Psychological Society. Available from: www.bps.org.uk/PTM-Main

None of this is to suggest that these problems never have organic components, or that the distinction between functional and organic is a fixed one. Survivors of childhood abuse and domestic violence, for example, may sustain neurological difficulties which can act as one of the maintaining factors for subsequent emotional or behavioural problems. More generally, physical illnesses, disabilities and developmental disorders have psychological and emotional consequences and meanings along with physiological effects. The PTM Framework can therefore be relevant to psychological distress accompanying medical, developmental or neurological conditions, whether as a result of coping with them or as the consequence of associated experiences of adversity. Similarly, there are implications for people with physical health conditions, since these are so often related to and accompanied by other adverse life experiences as well as being distressing in their own right.

As a separate issue, physical health problems can sometimes present as, or be wrongly identified as, mental health conditions. The wide and not always recognised range of possibilities includes hormonal imbalances, vitamin deficiencies, viral infections, autoimmune diseases, and so on. These conditions need detection and appropriate medical treatment, and are not part of the argument of this document.

It is essential to be explicit about these distinctions because there are important differences between forms of distress and troubling behaviour that are enabled and influenced by our biology – as all human experience is – as opposed to bodily and other problems where there is evidence for a primary causal role for biological disease processes or impairments in the major aspects of the difficulties. This document takes the position that the distinction is sufficiently valid to require different theoretical frameworks for each, as well as to inform research programmes and practice.

Finally, there is a large and growing literature on the potentially damaging effects, both mental and physical, of psychiatric drugs of all kinds. Professionals should be very aware of the possibility that these drugs may be causing or exacerbating emotional distress and physical disability. This too is beyond the scope of our argument, except in so far as adherence to the principles of the PTM Framework would be likely to lead to greatly reduced levels of prescribing.

Part 2: Overview of theory and research

Conclusions from the literature on the roles of social context and biology

The overwhelming support for the causal impact of relational and social adversities, mediated by bodily responses, in emotional distress and troubled or troubling behaviour, is summarised in the main publication*. Broad patterns of relationships between social, psychological and biological aspects of emotional distress, unusual experiences and troubled or troubling behaviour have been described by many researchers. This sets the scene for addressing the core question of this project:

> *How might these broad trends and relationships be used to delineate narrower, provisional general patterns which can inform our understanding of the particular difficulties of an individual, family or other group?*

To date, attempts to identify specific pathways or patterns have been hampered by three broad trends in the evidence which can be summarised as: *Everything causes everything; Everyone has experienced everything;* and *Everyone suffers from everything.* In summary, and as a generalisation, all types of adverse events and circumstance seem to raise the risk for all types of mental health presentations (as well as for criminal and offending behaviour, physical health problems, and a range of other problematic social outcomes). This appears to be mediated, for better or for worse, by all types of attachment relationships, and by all kinds of social support, biological mechanisms and emotional and cognitive styles.

This evidence emphasises the limitations of assuming causal pathways in which specific adversities or biological states are hypothesised to be associated with specific outcomes or 'disorders'. While producing some valuable insights, this kind of research does not take us very much further in understanding causal links between particular risk events (e.g. physical or sexual abuse, social deprivation) and particular outcomes or consequences (e.g. low mood, anxiety, eating problems, hearing voices). Some of these limitations can be attributed to the retention of diagnostic categories and the persistence of positivist assumptions, and the consequent downplaying of social, material and cultural contexts, along with marginalisation of the role of personal meaning and agency. In other words, this approach is still largely situated within the '*DSM* mindset'. It is also, therefore, limited in its ability to conceptualise causality and identify causal patterns in relation to the thoughts, feelings and behaviour of embodied human beings who are actively making sense of their lives in interdependence with their relational, social, cultural and spiritual environments.

The main publication presents an extensive discussion of the principles and research that offer philosophical, theoretical and empirical bases for moving beyond these limitations

---

* Johnstone, L. & Boyle, M. with Cromby, J., Dillon, J., Harper, D., Kinderman, P., Longden, E., Pilgrim, D. & Read, J. (2018). *The Power Threat Meaning Framework: Towards the identification of patterns in emotional distress, unusual experiences and troubled or troubling behaviour, as an alternative to functional psychiatric diagnosis.* Leicester: British Psychological Society. Available from: www.bps.org.uk/PTM-Main

and for identifying non-diagnostic, non-medicalised patterns in the emergence of psychological and emotional distress. Before describing in more detail how to move from broad trends and relationships to more specific patterns, we will briefly consider three other bodies of work that have attempted the same task.

Patricia Crittenden's Dynamic Maturational Model (DMM: 2002, 2005; 2006) synthesises sources from evolutionary biology, ethology, epigenetics, cognitive neuroscience, attachment theory, psychoanalysis and general systems theory, to conceptualise mental health problems in terms of attachment-based psychobiological response patterns. The DMM is an ambitious and inclusive framework that addresses the impact of interpersonal threat (ranging from overt abuse to less severe forms of adversity) on various aspects of human functioning.

Crittenden suggests that early attachment experiences produce emotional, behavioural, cognitive and somatic responses that are defensive and self-protective, and which are adapted throughout development to promote survival. The child will thus be likely to react to threat by reverting to particular 'dispositional representations' (i.e. 'patterns of neurological activity that dispose individuals to act in some manner': Damascio, quoted in Crittenden, 2005, p.3) which roughly correspond to attachment styles A, B or C. The representation process is the central mediating factor that results in the adoption of particular strategies – hence, the same experiences can lead to different outcomes in different individuals. She proposes that when certain adaptations extend beyond the original threatening circumstances in which they developed, they tend to be seen as 'pathological.' Current difficulties such as dissociation, 'paranoia', anxiety and so on are seen as former 'solutions' that have outlived their original usefulness.

Crittenden suggests the identification of 'functional formulation patterns' as an alternative to symptom-based diagnoses (Crittenden & Dallos, 2012, p.407). She elaborates on the basic A, B and C attachment patterns by positing a range of Type A and Type C strategies, more of which become available as the individual matures. For example, she suggests that 'Type A strategies' are based on the use of cognition in order to cope with threat, while minimising awareness of feelings. Depending on the degree of reliance on such strategies, the end result might range from mild emotional inhibition to more disabling problems such as 'depression' and 'psychosis.' 'Type C strategies' are triggered by strong emotions like anger and fear, as well as physical arousal (e.g. elevated heart rate) and a corresponding reduction in the capacity to use cognitive information to, for example, predict and estimate risk. In mild forms this type of strategy might cause problems with aggression or anxiety, and in stronger versions, result in states of extreme insecurity which may be diagnosed as 'paranoia', 'personality disorder' or eating problems. 'Type B strategies' are more likely to be associated with positive assumptions and representations about oneself, other people, and the world. These groupings describe relational styles and strategies for coping with threat and achieving safety in particular situations, not people themselves, or traits or characteristics residing within people.

The end result is an array of possible 'functional formulation patterns' that individuals may call upon in certain situations in order to predict, avoid or survive perceived or actual threat, and to maintain relationships. The DMM proposes that different responses (or in psychiatric terminology 'symptoms') may be utilised for similar protective purposes. Conversely, the same experiences ('symptoms') may not cluster together, because they may perform different functions for each person. The DMM also emphasises the importance of customising therapeutic interventions to each person's response set.

Crittenden and Dallos have attempted a synthesis between the DMM and systemic family therapy (Crittenden & Dallos, 2009) in order to understand how DMM strategies may be played out in mutually reinforcing ways within families. They emphasise that, like individuals, 'families are meaning making systems' (Crittenden & Dallos, 2012, p.402), and that these meanings are shaped by language and social discourses. Awareness of wider circumstances helps to decide whether intervention is best carried out at individual, family, community, and/or cultural political levels (p.406).

Paul Gilbert (2007) draws on evolutionary theory, neuroscience, and developmental and social psychology in order to propose a model that relates personal attributions, attachment styles, and biologically-based affect systems to different manifestations of low mood (and more recently to other presentations such as 'psychosis'). He posits that these mood states stem from evolved defence strategies that help us to negotiate interpersonal threat and loss, as well as other dangers. He suggests that in order to survive, we need to be able to elicit and give care; to co-operate with others; and to compete to win resources and find a place within the social group. Correspondingly we are primed to feel very distressed by disconnection, exclusion, and 'social defeat' – responses that may have parallels in animal behaviour.

Gilbert suggests that these defence strategies interact via affect regulation systems and in turn give rise to 'sequences of interacting processes that create complex biopsychosocial patterns' (Gilbert, 2007, p.17) based on broad meanings (for example, about whether others are safe). Affect regulation is said to occur through three main systems: (1) threat systems (associated with high arousal and emotions like anger, anxiety and disgust), (2) soothing/affiliative/ emotional regulation systems (associated with feelings of connectedness, safety, and contentment); and (3) drive/excitement systems (associated with rewards and goal-seeking, and feelings of energy and pleasure). Taken together, the three interacting drives are believed to shape subjective experiences and meanings of distress, partly though the activation of protection strategies (such as fight/flight/freeze, strive, protest and so on), partly by emotional memories and past experiences, and partly by current events.

In this model, adulthood wellbeing is significantly influenced by the 'emotional memories' that have been encoded in association with these three emotional drives, and early attachment experiences are believed to be a formative way of regulating them. For example, in an abusive or neglectful environment, drive-seeking and threat systems will be more readily rehearsed and activated while the capacity for self-soothing and affiliation will be inhibited. Our human capacity to think, reflect, interpret and use language and symbolism adds another layer of complexity which in turn feeds back into the response patterns in both adaptive and non-adaptive ways – for example, by strengthening or moderating our beliefs that we have been/will be abandoned, hurt, shamed, excluded, and so on.

Although these complex defence strategies may not always be experienced as positive, they are premised on the notion that individuals draw on familiar, learned adaptations to try and manage experiences of loss, rejection, or threat. As such, Gilbert shares Crittenden's view that these evolved survival strategies are essentially protective, although likely to be seen as 'pathological' if prolonged beyond the original circumstances. Similarly, he sees these strategies as potentially serving different purposes for different people. These dynamics exist within what Gilbert calls 'social and physical ecologies', which implies a need for interventions at systemic, social and political levels as well: 'Psychological models must address these issues (and questions of social justice) and not see problems in coping and thinking as personal deficits (rather than linked to protection strategies)' (Gilbert, 2007, p.106). His work thus conceptualises low mood (and potentially other forms of distress) within a broad context, and suggests practical and non-blaming explanatory frameworks for tailoring therapeutic interventions to the person's specific circumstances (e.g. reducing feelings of threat, disconnection, inferiority, and/ or shame; and the large literature on developing the capacity for self-compassion and self-soothing; for example, Lee & James, 2012).

The 'Trauma-informed approach' is based on the recognition that the majority of people using welfare services have experienced significant adversity and threat in their past and/or current lives (e.g. Sweeney et al., 2016; www.blueknot.org.au; www.acestoohigh. com). It argues that healing through having experiences witnessed and validated within trusting relationships is key to recovery. The core question is thus not 'What is wrong with you?' but 'What has happened to you?' (Blue Knot Foundation, 2012, p.14). In this document, these events and circumstances are generally referred to as 'adversities' to encompass the many forms that they can take. The resulting research unites evidence about the effects of threatening, traumatic and abusive experiences with what is known about human brain development, especially in the context of attachments and early relationships. This is a rapidly-expanding field, and there is now a very considerable body of evidence linking these experiences to a whole range of emotional, physical and social outcomes. In line with this, a growing number of mental health services have taken on elements of this perspective. Trauma-informed projects are also running in service design, education, prisons, and public health (examples at www.acestoohigh.com).

Work based on this approach has two linked aspects: ensuring that systems as a whole are 'trauma-informed', and offering trauma-specific interventions. The former implies that all staff will be trained to recognise and work with the effects of threat and adversity, and that all aspects of services will be designed to promote safety, choice and empowerment, and avoid re-traumatisation. The latter are typically based on the three-stage trauma-informed model, consisting of Safety/Stabilisation; Processing; and Integration (Blue Knot Foundation, 2012; Herman, 1992; Courtois & Ford, 2013; and see Chapter 8). The three-stage model thus offers an over-arching structure for therapeutic interventions from all modalities, along with other kinds of support as appropriate. It is important to note that there is no assumption that every service user will have a history of specific traumatic events, or that if they do, they will wish to address this directly. This is not 'one-size-fits-all', but a flexible, service-user-oriented approach based on awareness that adversity, broadly defined, is very likely to be part of the picture. Clearly this approach has generated important and innovative therapeutic work, and the general causal links between adversity and distress are indisputable. However, claims to have identified pathways between specific traumatic events and specific kinds of distress have very weak support, as would be predicted by the principles underpinning our proposed framework.

Overview of the models

There are significant areas of overlap between the models. Their strengths and limitations can be summarised as follows:

- Response patterns are not seen as pathological, but rather as adaptive reactions which may have outlived their usefulness. Furthermore, it is not assumed that response patterns are found solely in a particular group such as the 'mentally ill'; and nor do those so labelled rely on them all the time. Rather, we all employ a variety of strategies that may be more or less useful in particular situations. The implication is that 'co-morbidity' is not a nosological problem to be solved, but a reflection of the fact that people can use multiple ways to respond to adversity and threat.

- The models are able to accommodate heterogeneity because they allow for general, functional patterns of individual adaptation as opposed to hypothesising links between (specific) causal events and (specific) consequences or outcomes. The implication is that it will not be possible to identify universal aetiological causal pathways, nor to devise standardised packages of intervention linked to particular expressions of distress.

- The models incorporate a non-reductionist role for biology as mediator and enabler, and the core elements of the psychobiological response patterns are, unlike biomedical models, based on extensive evidence across a range of areas. In other words, they are 'psychobiosocial' in a sense that does not imply the primacy of (unevidenced) biological causal factors, contrary to most current uses of the term 'biopsychosocial' in relation to mental health. However, the assembly of these multiple factors into patterns, meanings and pathways is more speculative. Gilbert's three main affect-regulation system and his 'old brain/new brain' distinction is not universally accepted (Le Doux, 1999; Goldstein, 1995; Panksepp, 1988), while there are also critiques of aspects of attachment theory (see review by Cassidy & Shaver, 2008).

- The models suggest how response patterns can arise out of, and be co-created within, developmental and relational contexts. However, only the trauma-informed approach fully incorporates current evidence about the extremely high rates of adversity in those who access mental health and other welfare systems.

- All these models place a welcome emphasis on personal meaning and the importance of healing through relationships. Gilbert makes the most explicit links to wider power interests through social discourses about competition, status and so on (e.g. Gilbert, 2007). Integrating a family systems approach into the DMM promotes recognition of the need to address meaning at all levels of organisation from familial to political, cultural and societal (Crittenden & Dallos, 2009) in line with current family therapy traditions (Dallos & Stedmon, 2014). Overall, though, this is an aspect of the models which is relatively underdeveloped.

- Despite some acknowledgement of social, material and political contexts, the emphasis in both Gilbert's and Crittenden's work tends to be on solutions in terms of therapy (individual and family) rather than, or not supplemented by, self-help, community support, and other forms of social policy and action. The evidence supporting trauma-informed approaches has been applied more widely, and has also been influential on public health policy (www.acestoohigh.com; and see the main publication).

However, preventative work within this field generally stops short of challenging the discrimination, inequality, and socioeconomic structures that create the fundamental conditions within which adversities multiply.

- Trauma-informed approaches emphasise the importance of working with diversity (http://www.samhsa.gov/nctic/trauma-interventions). There are specific projects looking at, for example, the experience of intergenerational trauma in Aboriginal peoples in Canada (Arthur et al., 2013). Overall, though, the models give relatively little attention to cross-cultural influences on the experience and expression of distress, and the assumptions underpinning their work are primarily Western in origin. For example, it has become apparent that the shape, emergence and consequences of attachment relationships are far from universal and may present very differently in non-Western settings, implying the need for a more culturally-sensitive conceptualisation of how these developmental trajectories are played out (Otto & Keller, 2014).

- A major limitation from the perspective taken here is that the models are only partially successful in distancing themselves from diagnostic terms and assumptions. Gilbert's impressive body of work largely takes the diagnostic category 'depression' as a given (Gilbert, 2007). Although 'depression' has a lay meaning as well as a clinical one, this reification of meaningful response states is potentially unhelpful. Crittenden suggests the interesting possibility of 'functional formulation patterns' as an alternative to psychiatric diagnoses, but also uses terminology such as 'personality disorder', 'psychopathology' and so on. Leading practitioners of trauma-informed care still use diagnostic categories (see critique by Burstow, 2003) and attempted, unsuccessfully, to introduce new diagnostic categories of 'Complex Post Traumatic Disorder' into *DSM-IV* and 'Developmental Trauma Disorder' into *DSM-5* (Van der Kolk, 2014). While this was partly driven by the need to accommodate US insurance requirements (Wylie, 2010), the effect is to stop short of a fundamental rethink of the whole concept of psychiatric diagnosis.

In summary, then, the models collectively suggest a range of innovative and important perspectives on non-diagnostic conceptualisations of distress, which have valuable implications for practice and intervention. Their shared message, based on a considerable amount of evidence, is that the experiences usually described as 'symptoms' may be better understood as strategies for surviving adversity, rather than as 'psychiatric illnesses' or 'disorders'. At the same time, they fall short in various ways from presenting a comprehensive and conceptually coherent alternative to psychiatric diagnosis. As a result, there is a risk that these perspectives will be assimilated back into individualistic accounts of distress. There is a need for a more fundamental shift in thinking, as described below.

Part 3: The Power Threat Meaning Framework

An alternative basis for the identification of patterns in mental distress, unusual experiences and problematic behaviour

The principles and practices, theory and evidence summarised above are now synthesised in order to describe an alternative framework in more detail. Because of their importance, the key features of the framework are repeated here, and it is argued that any attempt to outline alternatives to the psychiatric diagnostic system should have the following characteristics:

- Be based on the identification of broad patterns and regularities in the expression and experience of distress and troubled or troubling behaviour, as opposed to specific biological (or psychological) causal mechanisms linked to discrete disorder categories.
- Show how these patterns are evident to varying degrees and in varying circumstances for all individuals across the lifespan.
- Not assume 'pathology'; rather, describe coping and survival mechanisms which may be more or less functional as an adaptation to particular conflicts and adversities in both the past and present.
- Integrate the influence of biological/genetic and epigenetic/evolutionary factors in mediating and enabling these response patterns.
- Integrate relational, social, cultural and material factors as shaping the emergence, persistence, experience and expression of these patterns.
- Account for cultural differences in the experience and expression of distress.
- Assign a central role to personal meaning, emerging out of social and cultural discourses and belief systems, material conditions and bodily potentialities.
- Assign a central role to personal agency, or the ability to exercise influence within inevitable psychosocial, biological and material constraints (especially if supported within healing relationships and communities).
- Acknowledge the centrality of the relational/social/political context in decisions about what counts as a 'mental health' need or crisis in any given case.
- Provide an evidence base for drawing on these patterns in order to inform individual/ family/group narratives.
- Offer alternative ways of fulfilling the service-related, administrative and research functions of diagnosis.
- Suggest alternative language uses, while arguing that there can be no one-to-one replacements for current diagnostic terms.
- Include meanings and implications for action in a wider community/social/political context.

The main publication* collectively summarises evidence on fundamental aspects of the emergence of mental distress, unusual experiences and problematic behaviour as follows:

- The operation of **POWER** (in its various forms of biological/embodied power; coercive or power by force; legal power; economic and material power; social and cultural capital; interpersonal power; and ideological power). These manifestations of power, both negative and positive, operate through social structures, institutions and organisations; through our physical environment; through the media and education; and through social and family relations.

- The kinds of **THREAT** that the negative operation of power may pose to the individual, the group and the community, with particular reference to mental distress.

- The central role of **MEANING** (as produced within social and cultural discourses, and primed by evolved and acquired bodily responses) in shaping the operation, experience and expression of power, threat, and our responses to threat.

- The evolved and learned **THREAT RESPONSES,** mediated through meaning-based bodily capabilities, that any individual (or family, group or community) experiencing threat arising within the Power Threat Meaning process, may need to use to protect themselves. Rather than being 'diagnosed' as *passively suffering biological deficits,* we suggest that service users (and all of us) can be recognised and validated as *activating threat responses for protection and survival.* The experiences that are described as 'symptoms' are therefore better understood as reactions to threat, or 'survival strategies'.

In line with these analyses, a conceptual framework for the origins and persistence of distress, unusual experiences and troubled or troubling behaviour is now proposed, and is described as the **Power Threat Meaning (PTM) Framework.**

To put it at its simplest, the PTM Framework replaces 'What is wrong with you?' with four key questions:

- 'What has happened to you?' (How is **Power** operating in your life?)
- 'How did it affect you?' (What kind of **Threats** does this pose?)
- 'What sense did you make of it?' (What is the **Meaning** of these situations and experiences to you?)
- 'What did you have to do to survive?' (What kinds of **Threat Response** are you using?)

Translated into practice with an individual, family or group, two additional questions need to be asked:

- 'What are your strengths?' (What access to **Power resources** do you have?)
- ...and to integrate all the above: 'What is your story?'

(See Appendix 1 for suggestions about ways of adapting these questions for practice.)

The evidence cited in the main publication supports the contention that humans are social beings whose **core needs** include:

---

* Johnstone, L. & Boyle, M. with Cromby, J., Dillon, J., Harper, D., Kinderman, P., Longden, E., Pilgrim, D. & Read, J. (2018). *The Power Threat Meaning Framework: Towards the identification of patterns in emotional distress, unusual experiences and troubled or troubling behaviour, as an alternative to functional psychiatric diagnosis.* Leicester: British Psychological Society. Available from: www.bps.org.uk/PTM-Main

- To experience a sense of justice and fairness within their wider community.
- To have a sense of security and belonging in a family and social group.
- To be safe, valued, accepted and loved in their earliest relationships with caregivers.
- To meet basic physical and material needs for themselves and their dependants.
- To form intimate relationships and partnerships.
- To feel valued and effective within family and social roles.
- To experience and manage a range of emotions.
- To be able to contribute, achieve and meet goals.
- To be able to exercise agency and control in their lives.
- To have a sense of hope, belief, meaning and purpose in their lives.

…all of which will provide the conditions for them to be able to offer their children…

- Secure and loving early relationships as a basis for optimum physical, emotional and social development and the capacity to meet their own core needs.

Anything that prevents these core needs being met may be experienced as a threat to emotional, physical, relational and/or social safety and survival. As a result, human beings have evolved to be able to employ a range of threat responses which **serve the function of protection from core threats.**

The PTM Framework therefore fulfils the following main purposes:

- Highlighting the common meaning-based threats posed by various manifestations of power.
- Highlighting the evolved and acquired strategies commonly employed to counteract these threats.
- Highlighting the links between threats and protective threat responses that have been obscured by the use of diagnostic labels.
- In the place of traditional psychiatric models, providing a basis for identifying broad, evidence-based patterns that synthesise the influences of Power, Threat, Meaning and associated Threat Responses.
- Utilising these patterns to generate personal, group and/or social narratives that help to restore meaning and agency, in line with the relevant cultural assumptions, and along with this, have the potential to create hope, rebuild relationships, and promote social action.

It is important to note that we are conceptualising this framework in a fundamentally different way from the more traditional biopsychosocial model:

- Although a tripartite model is a convenient heuristic, the three elements are not independent, but evolve out of each other. There is no actual divide either within or across the proposed core aspects. The person does not exist, and cannot be understood, separately from his/her relationships, community and culture; meaning only arises out of the interaction of social, cultural and biological elements; and biological capacities cannot be separated from the social and interpersonal environment.
- Unlike (some versions of) biopsychosocial models, there is no assumption of pathology, and the 'biological' aspects are not privileged. Rather, biological aspects constitute one level of explanation, arising out of and shaped by all the others
- The capacities for creating meaning (within available discourses) and the exercise of agency (within material and biosocial restraints and cultural understandings) are fundamental attributes of human beings. Personal meanings are not simply freely chosen

but are reflective of experience, relationships and wider social and cultural circumstances. 'Meaning' is intrinsic to the expression and experience of all forms of emotional distress, giving both shared and unique shape to the individual's personal responses.

- While most mental health (and related) work is aimed at the individual, we argue that meaning and distress must also be understood at social, community and cultural levels. Thus we see the PTM Framework as applying equally to understanding, intervention and social action in a wider sense. In other words, the Framework aligns with a recent UN report recommending a shift of focus towards '"power imbalance" rather than "chemical imbalance"' (UNHRC, 2017, p.19).

Part 4 demonstrates how the threat reactions and survival strategies that arise within a Power Threat Meaning context can be tentatively grouped into broad, provisional, probabilistic, evidenced **patterns of meaning-based threat responses to power.** These responses, and the patterns of which they form a part can be described by verbs that will be as near as we can come to replacing diagnostic terms. *'Reconfigured as verbs, diagnostic categories become strategies for living'* (Laura Kerr on dxsummit.org). The proposed patterns are thus conceptually very different from diagnostic clusters.

One important implication of the principles outlined above is that they suggest a potential solution to the hitherto irresolvable dilemma about the application of Western psychiatric classification systems to non-Western cultures and expressions of distress, both within the UK and around the world (for further discussion of ethnicity and culture, see Chapters 2, 3 and 4 of the main publication). The PTM Framework predicts and allows for the existence of widely varying cultural experiences and expressions of distress without positioning them as bizarre, primitive, less valid, or as exotic variations of the dominant diagnostic or other Western paradigms. The same applies to historical phenomena such as 'hysteria'. Viewed as a meta-framework that is based on universal evolved human capabilities and threat responses, the basic principles of the PTM Framework apply across time and across cultures. Within this, open-ended lists of threat responses and functions (described later) allow for an indefinite number of locally and historically specific expressions of distress, all shaped by prevailing cultural meanings.

The Foundational Power Threat Meaning pattern that arises out of the various elements of the PTM Framework will now be described. This pattern underpins the specific patterns described later on, by summarising regularities in the experience and expression of distress at the most general level.

The Foundational Power Threat Meaning Pattern

In order to identify meaningful patterns in distress within the trends and regularities described in detail in the main publication, the starting point needs to be the most general foundational pattern which underpins all the others, whether applied at an individual, family, group or population level. The Foundational Pattern described below uses the PTM Framework to synthesise the extensive amount of research and evidence into the whole range of social and interpersonal adversities discussed in the main publication. This suggests a summary of population-level trends and regularities as follows:

- All forms of adversity are more common within contexts of inequality and other forms of deprivation, discrimination, marginalisation and social injustice.

- Social discourses and ideological meanings shape the experience and expression of distress.
- Disrupted early attachment relationships are a form of adversity in themselves, and also set the scene for biologically-mediated emotional responses to subsequent adversities.
- A large part of the impact of adversity can be accounted for by factors which exacerbate the experience of threat. These include younger developmental age; entrapment; interpersonal and intentional threat; unpredictability and lack of control over the threat; repeated and multiple threats; physical invasiveness; chronic background threat; and lack of someone to confide in and act as protector.
- Ameliorating factors such as later developmental stage, having someone to confide in, being able to escape, are the opposite of the exacerbating ones (see Box 1, Exacerbating aspects of adversities).

Box 1: Exacerbating aspects of adversities

- Early developmental stage
- Lack of person to support/confide in/protect
- Multiple kinds of danger
- Long-lasting/repeated danger
- Severity of the danger
- Escapability or 'trappedness'
- Lack of predictability and control over the threat
- Physical invasiveness of the threat
- Closeness in time/Co-occurrence to other threats
- Threat to sense of self
- Interpersonal and intentional threat
- Sense of betrayal by individuals or institutions
- Perceived social threat
- Greater number of perpetrators
- Threat that occurs within an emotional or attachment relationship
- Chronicity, background threat, either environmental or personal

There is robust evidence to show that these factors increase the likelihood of emotional damage in the face of threats and adversities. These are not specific threats in themselves, but are *aspects of threatening situations* that *exacerbate* the experience of threat. Their opposites – e.g. later developmental stage, having someone to confide in, being able to escape – will, other things being equal, *reduce* the experience and impact of threat.

In addition:

- *The impact of adversities is cumulative.* There is a clear dose-effect, and as adversities multiply, the negative outcomes (biological, psychological and social) increase in a graded fashion.
- *Experiencing one or more adversities increases the risk of experiencing subsequent adversities.* This means that simple patterns – single threat to single threat response – will be relatively rare in service settings.
- *The impact of adversities is synergistic.* The combined effect of more than one adversity is usually greater than, and may be qualitatively different from, the sum of their individual effects.

- *The more adversities someone experiences, the more kinds of threat responses they will use.* In these circumstances people will need to draw upon a greater number of survival strategies, reflected in the application of multiple psychiatric diagnoses.
- *Some threat responses, such as those diagnosed as 'psychosis', become more common along with the cumulative and synergistic effects of adversities* and can therefore be regarded as reflecting a greater degree of damage.
- The impacts of adversity may be *transmitted down the generations,* thus perpetuating these destructive cycles.
- Finally, *mental health and other human systems are often traumatising and re-traumatising in themselves,* setting up further cycles of cumulative and synergistic events in which diagnosis can act to confirm feelings of shame, deficit and exclusion, and admissions, labels and interventions may multiply.

Putting all this together results in what can be described as the Foundational Power Threat Meaning Pattern in mental distress and other behavioural, health and social outcomes.

The narrative summary of the Foundational Pattern is as follows:

> *Economic/social inequalities and ideological meanings which support the negative operation of power result in increased levels of insecurity, lack of cohesion, fear, mistrust, violence and conflict, prejudice, discrimination, and social and relational adversities across whole societies. This has implications for everyone, and particularly those with marginalised identities. It limits the ability of caregivers to provide children with secure early relationships, which is not only distressing in itself for the developing child, but may compromise their capacity to manage the impact of future adversities. Adversities are correlated, such that their occurrence in a person's past and/or present life increases the likelihood of experiencing subsequent ones. Aspects such as intentional harm, betrayal, powerlessness, entrapment and unpredictability increase the impact of these adversities, and this impact is not just cumulative but synergistic. Over time, the operation of complex interacting adversities results in a greatly increased likelihood of experiencing emotional distress and troubled or troubling behaviours. The form of these expressions of distress is shaped by available resources, social discourses, bodily capacities and the cultural environment, and their core function is to promote emotional, physical and social safety and survival. As adversities accumulate, the number and severity of these responses rises in tandem, along with other undesirable health, behavioural and social outcomes. In the absence of ameliorating factors or interventions, the cycle is then set up to continue through further generations.*

Put like this, the outcomes seem hardly surprising. Nevertheless, it is important to have research-based confirmation of this common sense conclusion, because it is fundamentally opposed to the diagnostically-based one. It demonstrates that psychological and emotional distress is, like all human experience, mediated by biology but not in any simplistic sense caused by it. It illustrates the fact that emotional distress and troubling or troubled behaviour are on a spectrum, in which everyone is likely to be impacted by the consequences of social injustice as reflected through taken-for-granted aspects of everyday life, even if they have not experienced specific traumatic events. For the less fortunate or privileged, it illustrates how extreme and disabling circumstances can lead to extreme and disabling responses, in a predictable ratio to damage. It also suggests that there can be ways to escape the cycle, even in the most challenging contexts. The pattern is summarised in diagrammatic form in Figure 1.

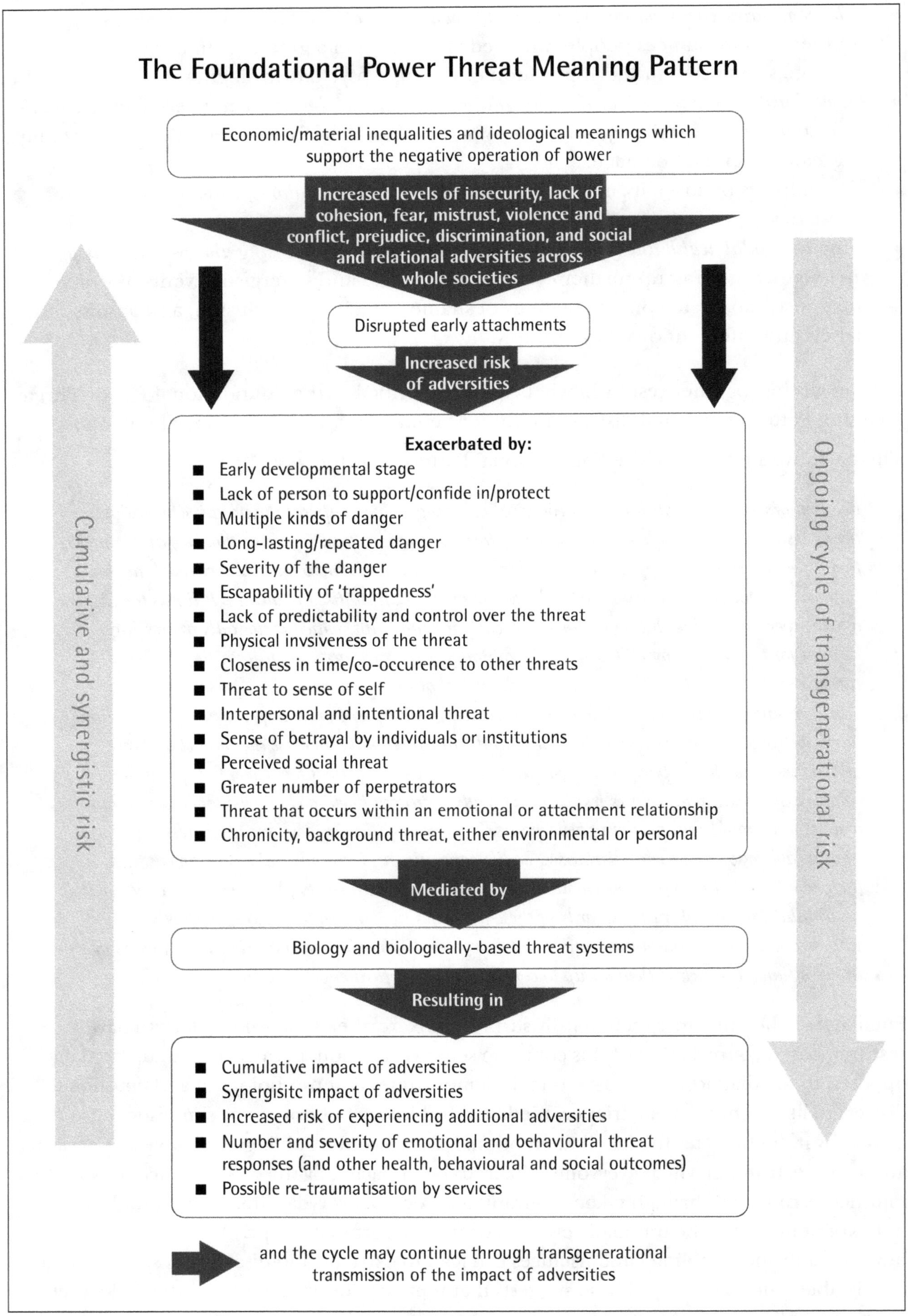

The Foundational Power Threat Meaning Pattern

Economic/material inequalities and ideological meanings which support the negative operation of power

Increased levels of insecurity, lack of cohesion, fear, mistrust, violence and conflict, prejudice, discrimination, and social and relational adversities across whole societies

Disrupted early attachments

Increased risk of adversities

Exacerbated by:

- Early developmental stage
- Lack of person to support/confide in/protect
- Multiple kinds of danger
- Long-lasting/repeated danger
- Severity of the danger
- Escapabilitiy of 'trappedness'
- Lack of predictability and control over the threat
- Physical invsiveness of the threat
- Closeness in time/co-occurence to other threats
- Threat to sense of self
- Interpersonal and intentional threat
- Sense of betrayal by individuals or institutions
- Perceived social threat
- Greater number of perpetrators
- Threat that occurs within an emotional or attachment relationship
- Chronicity, background threat, either environmental or personal

Mediated by

Biology and biologically-based threat systems

Resulting in

- Cumulative impact of adversities
- Synergisitc impact of adversities
- Increased risk of experiencing additional adversities
- Number and severity of emotional and behavioural threat responses (and other health, behavioural and social outcomes)
- Possible re-traumatisation by services

and the cycle may continue through transgenerational transmission of the impact of adversities

Cumulative and synergistic risk

Ongoing cycle of transgenerational risk

Figure 1: The Foundational Power Threat Meaning Pattern

Comments on the Foundational Power Threat Meaning Pattern

These are population-level trends and not pre-determined individual pathways, and they describe risks not inevitabilities. Nevertheless, the Foundational Pattern has extremely important implications for mental health systems and human services as a whole. A cumulative and synergistic model of the impact of adversities does not support the individualisation of distress, either medically or psychologically. Instead, it implies the need for action, primarily through social policy, at the earliest possible point, before the destructive and self-perpetuating cycle is set in motion.

The origins of the 'everythings…' problem can be clearly seen. The experience of adversities, especially in early years, sets up highly complex, overlapping, meaning-based, cumulative and synergistic patterns in which causality is contingent and probabilistic. The number of possible combinations of response (whether officially designated as 'pathological' or not) is almost infinite. The discrete causal pathways implied by psychiatric diagnosis do not and cannot exist in relation to human responses to adversity. Equally importantly, nor can we expect to find psychosocial versions of those pathways in terms of specific event to specific outcome. The Foundational Pattern, then, does not solve the 'everythings' problem. Rather, it acknowledges that this is how things are. This is an essential and long overdue recognition.

While many people who have been psychiatrically labelled will have experienced both attachment disruptions and specific forms of adversity, even the most loving and secure upbringing cannot provide protection against all threats, especially given a wider context of social inequality. Equally, very few people, whatever their early background, will survive circumstances such as domestic abuse, trafficking, refugee status, chronic physical pain and ill health, multiple bereavement, major natural disaster, war, captivity and so on, without emotional scars. The fewer ameliorating factors in a person's life (e.g. alternative caregivers; social support; adequate housing; skills and abilities; education; access to resources; appropriate intervention) the smaller the chance of escaping this cycle. However, it is just as important to recognise that each of these possibilities can also be played out positively – perhaps in the form of a caring relative, a particular talent, or a change in social circumstances. With the right kind of support, many people have been able to find a way out from these destructive patterns.

The Foundational Pattern arises in the context of the negative impacts of power, both immediate and more distant. Along with the work of many others, this analysis suggests that socioeconomic structures influence the social discourses and meanings which serve and shape the interests of various kinds of power, in both its negative and its positive operation. In all these situations, the individual's distress is likely to be increased in proportion to the extent to which they have assimilated the underlying social norms and discourses, for example those relating to appropriate gender roles or personal responsibility. Shame is a social emotion, and while a psychiatric diagnosis is sometimes welcomed as offering protection from shame for one's actions, it can also be experienced as shorthand for a community judgement of: 'You are a flawed and unacceptable member of the social group.' Diagnosis can thus set the scene for perpetuating the cycle of traumatisation, discrimination and social exclusion.

The Foundational PTM Pattern can be used in combination with an 'ameliorating factors' list as a quick checklist to suggest a way of understanding and validating the degree of distress/difficulty in functioning experienced by a particular individual, family, group or community. While the PTM Framework and the Foundational PTM Pattern can be used as they stand, they can also be seen as a meta-framework within which existing models and bodies of evidence can be accommodated. Additionally, they can serve as a reference point for identifying gaps in current theory and practice, which very often arise out of insufficient attention to the negative operation of power and its associated ideological meanings.

The next section outlines provisional General Patterns within the Foundational Power Threat Meaning Pattern.

Part 4: Provisional General Patterns arising out of the Foundational Pattern

This section illustrates how the four main elements of Power, Threat, Meaning and Threat Response can be used to identify patterns and regularities within the overarching Foundational Pattern. These regularities can be understood as more specific examples of **patterns of meaning-based threat responses to power.**

Towards the end of the section, there will be a demonstration of how these provisional, probabilistic, evidenced General Patterns within the Foundational one can serve as a basis for generating personal, group and/or social and community narratives that promote meaning and agency, and along with this, have the potential to create hope, rebuild relationships, and support social action. The Framework and General Patterns can also be used for the more effective fulfilment of the other claimed functions of psychiatric diagnosis, such as indicating interventions, planning services, making administrative decisions, and providing a basis for research (as described in the main publication*).

Before outlining the General Patterns, it is important to discuss in more detail what might be meant by a 'pattern' in this context, and the similarities and differences between these proposed patterns and the ones that are used to support medical diagnoses.

What is a pattern?

At the most general level, a pattern refers to associations that seem to occur above chance level, amongst whatever phenomena are under consideration. This meaningfulness of certain associations can be suggested by, for example, their high frequency of occurrence, by some evidence of causality, i.e. antecedent/consequence relationships, and by knowledge of processes which help make sense of them. The main publication describes how, in medicine, patterns or regularities of this sort in bodily functions, serve as 'templates' to which clinicians try to match an individual's bodily complaints and so gain some understanding of how these complaints have come about and might be alleviated. We also noted that these patterns are at very different levels of complexity and development, providing varying levels of understanding of an individual's problems.

The difficulties of deriving a specific definition of 'pattern' in this kind of context are well illustrated in a classic paper on medical diagnosis by Engle and Davis published in 1963 but just as relevant today (see e.g. Rosenberg, 2002). The similarities between the aims of medical diagnosis and the aims of alternatives to psychiatric diagnosis mean that the general arguments are relevant to discussion of patterns of emotional and behavioural difficulties as well.

Engle and Davis (1963) describe medical diagnoses as being at different 'orders of certainty' reflecting the different characteristics of the patterns they are based on and how

---

* Johnstone, L. & Boyle, M. with Cromby, J., Dillon, J., Harper, D., Kinderman, P., Longden, E., Pilgrim, D. & Read, J. (2018). *The Power Threat Meaning Framework: Towards the identification of patterns in emotional distress, unusual experiences and troubled or troubling behaviour, as an alternative to functional psychiatric diagnosis.* Leicester: British Psychological Society. Available from: www.bps.org.uk/PTM-Main

'certain' a clinician can be that a patient's presenting problems 'match' any particular general pattern. The first order of certainty includes presentations where the causes are usually very clear and specific and where there is very little variation from person to person or environment to environment. This would include frostbite, crush injuries and some other traumatic outcomes. At the other extreme, at the fifth order of certainty on Engle and Davis' scale, are constellations of signs and symptoms whose causes are not known and where there is a good deal of variability from person to person. In between are patterns with more or less well-defined links between causes and outcomes and/or more or less variation in individual presentations.

It might be argued that psychiatric diagnoses simply occupy a low point on this scale, but this is not the case. For all the reasons discussed in Chapter 1 of the main publication, the *DSM* and *ICD* clusters on which functional psychiatric diagnoses are based do not reach even Engle and Davis' lowest order of certainty – constellations of signs and symptoms – although common misuse of the terms 'sign' and 'syndrome' in discussions of psychiatric diagnosis might suggest otherwise.

Engle and Davis make several important points about general medical patterns and their role in understanding individual problems. First, the patterns and their separation one from another, are always provisional. We can point to some evidence of their validity, but they are never fixed. Second, the patterns are of different types, based on different sorts of evidence, including anatomical changes, causal agents, genetic or biochemical abnormalities and so on. Third, each pattern is underpinned by complex theory and research about the nature of its 'elements' and their relationship, and this theory and research, too, is continually being modified. Finally, these patterns have varying relationships to our understanding of an individual's problems. In some, the match is clear and straightforward, in others it is more open-ended and uncertain.

It has been emphasised that the kind of patterns one would expect to find in people's emotional and behavioural difficulties, their causes and consequences, are very different from the kind of patterns of bodily problems which inform medical diagnosis, that they are subject to fundamentally different types of causal regularity, and so need to be based on very different theoretical assumptions. However, Engle and Davis' general points are relevant to the task of describing patterns we can draw on in understanding emotional and behavioural difficulties. Specifically, these regularities will not conform to a single, straightforward definition of 'pattern'. There can be varying kinds of evidence of their validity, including their basis in appropriate theoretical frameworks, frequent occurrence, evidence of cause/effect relationships and knowledge of possible underlying mechanisms, but the patterns, and their boundaries, are inevitably provisional and have an open-ended relationship to the problems of particular individuals or groups. Nevertheless, the particular patterns proposed in this document are marked by the striking consistency with which their elements emerge from diverse forms of research with population-wide and service user groups. This includes historical and theoretical analyses; demographic, survey, questionnaire, experimental and other quantitative research; qualitative analyses; and, not least, the large body of personal testimonies about distress and unusual experiences.

Describing meaningful associations: Threat and threat response links

The patterns that can be derived from the PTM Framework and the Foundational Pattern are based on restoring the links between meaning-based threats and meaning-based threat responses.

It is useful to remember that in some situations, these links are readily acknowledged. It hardly needs stating that death of a loved one is experienced as loss and commonly evokes a reaction of grief; absence of attachment figures is experienced as abandonment and leads to anxiety and searching in young children; threat to physical safety results in terror and a fight/flight/freeze reaction; and so on. However, we do not usually ascribe pathology where the immediate psychosocial causal event is obvious. Thus, the temporary madness of grief (weeping, despair, hearing or seeing the person who has died, insomnia, restlessness, inability to concentrate and so on) is not seen as a psychiatric illness even though this constellation of reactions would undoubtedly attract a diagnosis in the absence of an obvious cause. A frantic, weeping, clinging child is not thought to be experiencing a 'disorder' once we realise she has lost her mother in a crowd. A hyperalert, highly anxious soldier is not seen as having suddenly developed a 'mental illness' if he is actually facing combat. Similarly, researchers into 'paranoia' have commented that its well-established links to experiences of bullying, violence, discrimination and unsafe environments render it 'understandable, and, indeed, adaptive' (Shevlin et al., 2015, p.213). In general healthcare settings the link between threatening event and distress (e.g. receiving a terminal diagnosis, difficult childbirth) may also be obvious, although there may be less awareness about the triggering of pre-existing adversities.

Some of these links are acknowledged in psychiatric diagnoses such as 'PTSD', and interestingly, this appears to be part of a growing trend. *DSM-5* (APA, 2013) has re-assigned 'PTSD' from the general category of 'Anxiety Disorders' to a new chapter on 'Trauma and stressor-related disorders', which is described as 'unique within *DSM-5* for requiring the identification of a triggering external event'. It includes 'Reactive attachment disorder', 'Disinhibited social engagement disorder' (in *ICD* this is 'Disinhibited attachment disorder), 'Acute stress disorder', 'Adjustment disorder' along with other specified or non-specified 'trauma and stressor-related disorders'. 'RAD' is said to develop 'as a result of maltreatment and/or neglect'. Acute stress disorder follows 'exposure to actual or threatened death, serious injury, or sexual violation.' Adjustment disorder 'occurs within a month of a distressing event'. 'Disinhibited attachment disorder' is 'the result of social neglect'. In other words, in all of these diagnoses the 'symptoms' are explicitly described as threat response patterns to psychosocial events and circumstances; indeed, biological causes are exclusion criteria. This new chapter joins the *DSM* and *ICD* one on 'Dissociative Disorders' (including Dissociative Identity Disorder, Dissociative Amnesia, and Depersonalisation/Derealisation) as the only place in which 'disorders' are explicitly acknowledged as responses to adverse psychosocial events. The trend for framing psychiatric presentations as the consequences of psychosocial adversities, albeit within a 'disorder' framework with all its limitations, would have been even stronger had van der Kolk (2014) and colleagues' detailed proposals for the new categories of 'Complex trauma disorder' and 'Developmental disorder' to replace many uses of *DSM-IV* diagnoses been accepted.

Similarly, a new category of Complex Post-Traumatic Stress Disorder (Complex Trauma for short) is proposed for inclusion in *ICD-11*. This is defined as *'A disorder that may develop following exposure to an event or series of events of an extreme and prolonged or repetitive nature that are experienced as extremely threatening or horrific and from which escape is difficult or impossible (e.g. torture, slavery, genocide, prolonged domestic violence, repeated childhood sexual or physical abuse)'* (Maercker et al., 2013).

The argument of this document is that the great majority of the experiences that are described as 'symptoms' of 'functional psychiatric disorders' (and many other problems, including some examples of criminal behaviour) can be understood in this way, but with no assumption of 'mental disorder', once the meaning-based threats have been identified and their links with the protective threat responses restored. The examples above also make it clear that responses need to be described at the level of *function*, not just at the level of behaviours and reactions that have usually been called 'symptoms'. The function of the child's crying is to attract the mother's attention; the function of the soldier's high arousal is to prepare for fight; the function of suspicious thoughts is to protect from attack; and so on.

A number of factors combine to ensure that these links are obscured in most of what is called 'mental illness', as well as in 'offending behaviour' and other health and social outcomes. Briefly summarised, these are:

- The threat (or operation of power) may be less obvious because it is subtle, cumulative, and/or socially acceptable. These factors obscure the negative operation of power and thus enable its perpetuation.
- The threat is often distant in time, even though the threat response is still active.
- The threats may be so numerous, and the responses so many and varied, that the connections between them are confused and obscured.
- There may be an accumulation of apparently minor threats and adversities over a very long period of time – particularly in older adults.
- The threat response may take an unusual or extreme form that is less obviously linked to the threat; for example, apparently 'bizarre' beliefs, hearing voices, self-harm, self-starvation.
- The person in distress may not be aware of the event(s) or the link themselves, since memory loss, dissociation and so on are part of their coping strategies.
- The person in distress might have become accustomed to disavowing the possibility of a link, because acknowledging it might have felt dangerous, stigmatising, shaming or in some other way unhelpful.
- The disavowing of these links may be encouraged by social discourses of blame, weakness, culpability and so on.
- Mental health professionals are socialised to obscure the link by the application of a diagnosis which imposes a powerful expert narrative of individual deficit and medical illness.
- There is resistance at all levels of society to recognising the prevalence of threats and the negative impacts of power.
- There are many vested personal, family, professional, organisational, community, business, economic and political interests in disconnecting threat from threat response and thus preserving the 'medical illness' model.
- The influences above combine to deprive people of a socially shared framework of thought within they can make sense of their own experiences in their own terms.

Cumulatively, these factors help to ensure that such experiences may 'take place outside the realm of socially validated reality' and thus become 'unspeakable' (Herman, 2001, p.8). This process, which has been described as 'betrayal blindness' (Freyd & Birrell, 2013), operates at multiple levels – personal, familial, institutional and societal. In Judith Herman's words, 'Repression, dissociation and denial are phenomena of social as well as individual consciousness' (Herman, 2001, p.9). The impact on the person who is diagnosed can be seen as a form of 'epistemic injustice' (Fricker, 2007), a concept which describes the process through which members of marginalised groups are deprived of the social resources to understand their experiences outside of the dominant discourses. This point will be revisited later.

Meanwhile it is important to stress that the relevant sections of *ICD* and *DSM* still conceptualise threat responses as discrete medical 'symptoms' or complaints. In contrast, PTM groups them in terms of the main **functions** they serve, which in turn link to core human needs to be protected, valued, exercise agency and control, find a place in the social group, and so on. These strategies cut across traditional boundaries of 'normal/abnormal'.

Box 2: Functional groupings of threat responses

Regulating overwhelming feelings	E.g. by dissociation, self-injury, memory fragmentation, bingeing and purging, differential memory encoding, carrying out rituals, intellectualisation, 'high' mood, low mood, hearing voices, use of alcohol and drugs, compulsive activity of various kinds, overeating, denial, projection, splitting, derealisation, somatic sensations, bodily numbing
Protection from physical danger	E.g. by hypervigilance, insomnia, flashbacks, nightmares, fight/flight/freeze, suspicious thoughts, isolation, aggression.
Maintaining a sense of control	E.g. by self-starvation, rituals, violence, dominance in relationships
Seeking attachments	E.g. by idealisation, appeasement, seeking care and emotional responses, use of sexuality
Protection against attachment loss, hurt and abandonment	E.g. by rejection of others, distrust, seeking care and emotional responses, submission, self-blame, interpersonal violence, hoarding, appeasement, self-silencing, self-punishment
Preserving identity, self-image and self-esteem	E.g. by grandiosity, unusual beliefs, feeling entitled, perfectionism, striving, dominance, hostility, aggression
Preserving a place within the social group	E.g. by striving, competitiveness, appeasement, self-silencing, self-blame
Meeting emotional needs/self-soothing	E.g. by rocking, self-harm, skin-picking, bingeing, alcohol use, over-eating, compulsive sexuality
Communication about distress, elicit care	E.g. by self-injury, unusual beliefs, voice-hearing, self-starvation
Finding meaning and purpose	E.g. by unusual beliefs, overwork, high moods

A non-exhaustive list of threat responses is given in Box 2. Everyone experiences or uses these various forms of reaction and behaviour at times, and this is not necessarily a problem. Many of them – such as seeking attachments - are simply part of being human. Thus, they do not always serve the function of protecting from threat, whether they fall into the social categories of 'normal' or even desirable (e.g. hard work) or 'pathological' (e.g. holding unusual beliefs, hearing voices.) However, especially if they do serve a threat response purpose, they may become problematic in their own right.

The function of specific threat responses will vary situation to situation and from person to person, although some within-culture commonalities can be expected. This is because, as discussed in the main publication, different cultures provide 'symptom pools' or culturally recognised ways of expressing distress. In addition, the same threat response may serve multiple purposes for a single individual. Thus, self-injury may be used simultaneously as self-punishment, communication, and release of feelings. All of these strategies may represent people's attempts – conscious or otherwise – to survive the negative impacts of power and adversity by using the resources available to them. Managing overwhelming feelings and memories is a central survival need in all forms of distress, and is therefore likely to engage a very wide range of threat responses.

Restoring the links between threats and threat responses within the PTM Framework

The PTM Framework offers a structure for restoring the links between meaning-based threats (such as betrayal, abandonment, physical danger) and meaning-based threat responses (such as hyper-vigilance, self-injury and carrying out rituals.) Placing all of these in the wider contexts of power and social/ideological meanings will help to identify some general, probabilistic and overlapping General Patterns and regularities within the Foundational PTM Pattern.

Figure 2 ('Power Threat Meaning Framework General Patterns Template') may help to illustrate this process. It offers an elaboration of the Foundational Power Threat Meaning Pattern. The main elements of the Foundational Pattern (Power, Threat, Exacerbating/ ameliorating factors and Threat responses) have been expanded in order to allow for a more detailed description of their various aspects. 'Mediating biological factors' could include not just biologically-based threat responses, but general factors such as hormonal changes, temperamental factors, the impact of food restriction or sleep deprivation, changes associated with ageing, and so on, along with the consequences of neurodevelopmental conditions, stroke or brain injury if relevant. The addition of 'Meaning and discourse' allows for closer consideration of the characteristic personal and social meanings through which threats may be experienced.

This expanded version of the Foundational Pattern elements can be used to support the identification of evidence-based, but overlapping and contingent, Provisional General Patterns within the Foundational one, as described in the next section 'Provisional General Patterns: Identifying the elements and building blocks.'

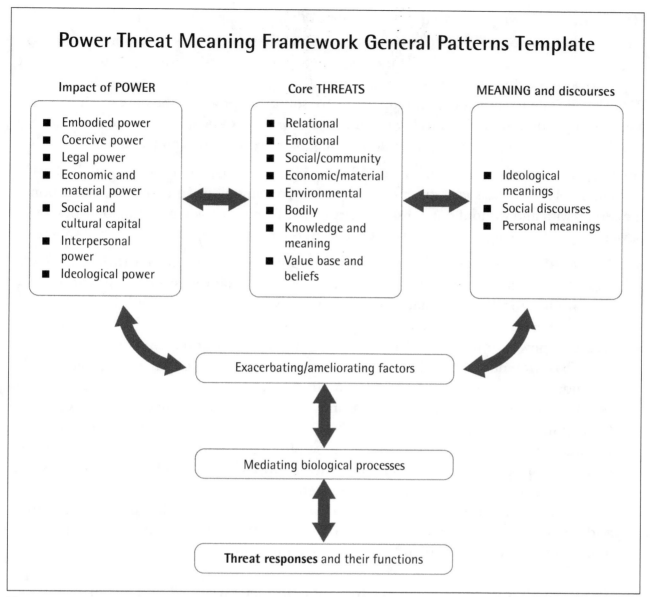

Power Threat Meaning Framework General Patterns Template

Impact of POWER

- Embodied power
- Coercive power
- Legal power
- Economic and material power
- Social and cultural capital
- Interpersonal power
- Ideological power

Core THREATS

- Relational
- Emotional
- Social/community
- Economic/material
- Environmental
- Bodily
- Knowledge and meaning
- Value base and beliefs

MEANING and discourses

- Ideological meanings
- Social discourses
- Personal meanings

Exacerbating/ameliorating factors

Mediating biological processes

Threat responses and their functions

Figure 2: Power Threat Meaning Framework General Patterns Template

Provisional General Patterns: Identifying the elements and building blocks

This section establishes a preliminary, evidence-based set of building blocks within the four aspects of Power, Threat, Meaning and Threat Response. These building blocks are then used as a basis for outlining General Patterns within the Foundational PTM one.

These lists are not exhaustive, in whatever cultural setting they are used. They are intended to be and to remain open-ended, in order to allow for evolving expressions of distress within particular local and historical contexts. Equally, ongoing research is needed for further confirmation of the validity and practical usefulness of the various elements.

It cannot be over-emphasised that the four aspects of Power, Threat, Meaning and Threat Response are inseparable, conceptually and experientially, although they are considered separately for the purposes of explanation and clarity.

There will now be a more detailed consideration of each of these four aspects.

POWER How is Power operating in your life? ('What has happened to you?')

Power can operate positively, in terms of protection, support and access to resources, and also negatively. It is impossible to describe the negative operation of power without at the same time implying both the threat that may result and the meaning that may be intrinsic to the threat. PTM's explicit delineation of the multiple possible sources of power in the life of a child/adult/group/community is central to making coherent sense of people's experiences, and should be the starting point for any understanding of distress or disturbing conduct.

Power operates though both immediate and more distant factors, mediated through bodily capacities, relationships, social structures, institutions, organisations and everyday interactions. It operates with and without our conscious awareness. There is no agreed listing of 'types' of power but the following conveys many aspects of its operation in separate but related spheres:

- **Biological or embodied power** operates both positively and negatively through embodied attributes and their cultural meanings: for example strength, physical appearance, fertility, skin shade and colour, embodied talents and abilities, and physical health and wellbeing.

- **Coercive power or power by force** is inevitably part of war and combat but also involves any use of violence, aggression, threats or greater physical strength, to frighten, intimidate or ensure compliance. Although often negative, coercive power can be used positively, for example when parents remove young children from danger.

- **Legal power** may also involve coercion, such as power of arrest, imprisonment or hospitalisation. It also refers to a wide range of rules and sanctions which regulate and control many areas of our lives and behaviour, support or limit other aspects of power, offer or restrict choices, protect people's rights, maintain social order, and so on.

- **Economic and material power** involves having the means to obtain valued possessions and services, to control others' access to them and to pursue valued activities. This applies in multiple areas including housing, employment, transport, education, medical treatment, leisure, legal services, safety and security, and privacy.

- **Social or cultural capital** refers to a form of power characterised by a mix of valued qualifications, social identities, knowledge and social connections which can be passed indirectly to the next generation. Increasingly this involves access to and skills in using computers, social media and other new technologies as well as understanding how they can shape our lives, for good or ill.

- **Interpersonal power** Although all forms of power can operate through relationships, this refers more specifically to the power to look after/not look after or protect someone, to help or abandon/leave them, to give/withdraw/withhold love and care, to undermine or support others in the development of their beliefs and identities, and so on.

- **Ideological power** involves control of meaning, language and 'agendas'. It also includes power to create narratives which support particular social and economic interests, to create beliefs or stereotypes about particular groups, to interpret your own or others' experience, behaviour and feelings and have these meanings validated by others, and the power to silence or undermine. It is one of the more hidden forms of power and operates across many areas including the media, advertising, government, education, the legal system, healthcare, science and research. Social media and the internet have allowed an increasingly pervasive and sophisticated operation of ideological power in ways that are often beyond our knowledge, awareness or skills.

As discussed in detail in the main publication, the negative operation of power in these closely related spheres, and the lack of socially valued attributes and resources, can produce challenging and threatening contexts and at the same time limit people's ability to respond to these threats.

THREAT What kinds of threat does it pose? ('How did it affect you?')

Threat describes the risk/dangers that the negative uses of power, as outlined above, may pose to the safety and survival of individuals and/or groups. Since the three aspects of Power, Threat and Meaning are interwoven, a list of threats inevitably implies both their origins and their meanings.

In situations such as natural disasters, the influence of power is more indirect and may be evident through, for example, differing opportunities to take preventative measures beforehand or access material support afterwards. In addition, all of us are vulnerable to experiencing random and unavoidable threats such as unexpected bereavement, accidents or physical ill-health. Here again, power will mainly have its effects through access to support with these life events, and the extent to which our early lives have equipped us to manage their emotional impact.

Core Threats to safety, survival or wellbeing can be conceived of as the opposite of the core human needs outlined earlier, and include:

Relational: e.g. disrupted attachments, abandonment, betrayal, isolation, shaming and humiliation, rejection, hostility, neglect, bereavement, lack of protection, entrapment, threats to boundaries, autonomy/control, self-concept and identity formation, invalidation.

Emotional: feeling emotionally overwhelmed and unsafe.

Social/community: e.g. isolation, exclusion, hostility, social defeat, injustice/unfairness, loss of social or work role.

Economic/material: e.g. poverty, inability to meet basic physical needs, or access basic services for oneself and/or dependants.

Environmental: e.g. lack of safety, physical threat, entrapment, loss of connection with homeland or the natural world.

Bodily: e.g. ill-health, chronic pain, bodily disability, injury, loss of function, physical danger, starvation, exhaustion, bodily invasion.

Knowledge and meaning construction: Lack of opportunity, support or social resources to access and use important sources of information and make sense of one's experiences; devaluing of one's own knowledges, understandings and experiences due to unequal power relations; imposition of meanings by social discourses and by more powerful others.

Identity: Lack of support to develop one's own identity; loss of social, cultural or spiritual identity; the adoption or imposition of devalued, subordinate or shameful identities relating to oneself or one's social group.

Value base: loss of purpose, values, beliefs and meanings; loss of community rituals, belief systems and practices.

Box 3: Meanings

MEANING – what is the Meaning of these situations and experiences to you? ('What sense did you make of it?')	
Unsafe, afraid, attacked	Trapped
Abandoned, rejected	Defeated
Helpless, powerless	Failed, inferior
Hopeless	Guilty, blameworthy, responsible
Invaded	Betrayed
Controlled	Shamed, humiliated
Emotionally overwhelmed	Sense of injustice/unfairness
Emotionally 'empty'	Sense of meaninglessness
Bad, unworthy	Contaminated, evil
Isolated, lonely	Alien, dangerous
Excluded, alienated	Different, 'abnormal'

As already noted, the threatening impacts of the operation of power cannot be understood without attention to their meaning for the individual and/or the social group. The operation of power (e.g. through abuse) does not necessarily imply a lasting threat to the individual (e.g. shame) if s/he has support to shape the meaning of the event (e.g. 'It was not your fault'). Conversely, an attribution of meaning may create a sense of threat even in the absence of current danger, as seen in some instances of suspicious thoughts ('paranoia'). 'Meaning' is thus the thread that holds all the other aspects of the PTM Framework together.

As discussed in the main publication, 'Meaning' is understood here as being constituted socially, relationally and personally through both beliefs and feelings, as well as through bodily reactions. Shame, for example, is constituted of both an embodied feeling, and a belief about oneself, as are fear, humiliation, failure, worthlessness, and so on.

At the pre-reflective end, certain meanings ('this person is safe/unsafe'; 'I am protected/ in danger') may be biologically primed as part of an evolved response pattern. At earlier developmental stages, meanings may be coded pre-consciously in the form of 'emotional memories' (Gilbert, 2007), images, symbols, bodily reactions and other non-verbal memory forms, and these are sometimes the first or main intimations of unresolved conflicts or adversities. With the development of language and reflective/mentalising ability comes the possibility of appraising and modifying existing meanings and creating new ones, shaped by social discourses and coded linguistically. However, non-verbal expressions of meaning including dreams, visions, bodily experiences such as tension, pain, discomfort and so on, continue to operate throughout our lives. Meaning can thus be communicated through behaviour, symbols and bodily reactions, as well as verbally. Sometimes these non-verbal or pre-verbal communications are accorded more respect and attention in non-Western cultures, and are thus less likely to be seen as pathology, 'disorder' or madness.

Language-based responses such as imagining, anticipating, ruminating, reflecting, interpreting, evaluating can all interact positively or negatively with other responses. Sometimes people will inadvertently set up reinforcing cycles of meaning which feed back into the threat responses, and create self-fulfilling prophecies. Alternatively, our reflective language-based abilities can be used to create new narratives and meanings that will help free us from these cycles.

THREAT RESPONSES What kinds of Threat Response are you using? ('What did you have to do to survive?')

The main publication supplies a very detailed consideration of the role of biology. The following section, however, focuses on embodied reactions which can be thought of more specifically as threat responses.

Faced with threat, human beings can draw upon a spectrum of threat responses in order to ensure emotional, physical, relational and social survival in the face of the negative impact of power. In other words, as emphasised above, these responses perform certain common *functions* which do not necessarily line up with existing 'symptom' descriptions or categories.

In the face of threat, people may call on any combination of these embodied responses (see Boxes 4–8) depending on the power resources and cultural meanings available to them. The responses listed first are those that are more pre-reflective and do not necessarily depend upon linguistic or consciously enacted strategies and resources, although they can be shaped by later learning. They may dominate at earlier developmental stages, although they are found throughout the lifespan, and may be more invariant across cultures.

The higher-order social-cognitive capabilities listed later are more dependent upon language and learning, and the person's characteristic pattern of strategies may involve more conscious awareness and selection. These are likely to appear later in developmental terms, to be more open to shaping by local meanings, and hence to be more culture-specific. Importantly, however, there is no absolute distinction between pre-reflective and reflective responses. Equally, there is no implied division into 'positive' versus 'negative' or 'mature' versus 'primitive' responses. All of these responses are adaptive in some circumstances and less so in others, particularly if used with a lack of flexibility.

Responses are conceived in terms of meaningful activity rather than mechanised or unthinking behaviour. This is does not mean that the responses are always consciously and deliberately chosen. Rather, it is to emphasise that they arise flexibly, in association with dynamic patterns of complex meaning, rather than automatically by association with stimuli whose meanings are more-or-less constant.

At the pre-reflective end, threat responses may be dominated by biologically-primed meanings/emotional aspects; for example, 'fight' with anger, 'flight' with fear. Distress and the emergence of memories may thus be experienced, particularly in the case of very severe or early adversities, in the form of overwhelming and frightening bodily reactions. However, in practice, responses from the start of the list will frequently draw on elements of language when they are enacted. Likewise, responses from the end of the list, although based on language, learning, discourse, narrative, symbols and self-representations, are always shaped by elements of meaning derived from pre-reflective feelings. In any case, what is reflected upon in one moment can fall into the pre-reflective 'background' of activity in the next. Similarly, a previously obscure meaning can suddenly emerge and become prominent. These shifts in the extent and manner of the reflections and interpretations people make of their own experiences add further layers of complexity and contingency to their response patterns. Additional shaping comes from others' responses, available social meanings, and access to power resources.

A key consideration from an intervention perspective is whether the threat responses are adaptive in their current circumstances. This raises the wider question of how far our attention should be directed towards the responses, and how far towards the circumstances which give rise to them. It also raises the question of who is distressed or disturbed by the threat responses, and why. (NB: It is acknowledged that particularly in criminal justice systems and mental health settings, there is a need to consider not just the adaptiveness of the response from the person's perspective, but its legality and potential harm to others).

Whether or not any specific reaction can be considered as a threat response depends on meaning and context; thus, there are many possible reasons for somatic experiences, dissociating, insomnia, using alcohol, isolating oneself, speech delay, and so on, and not all of them are threat-related. Particularly in specialties like Older Adult, Intellectual Disability and Neuropsychology, expressions of distress may be shaped by cognitive and other physical impairments. For example, in ID, some 'behavioural phenotypes' are associated with specific (often rare) neuro-developmental conditions such as Prader-Willi, Lesch-Nyan, Fragile X, etc. People diagnosed with 'autistic spectrum conditions' experience particular neurologically based difficulties, e.g. sensory processing, and are very vulnerable to experiencing sensory 'overload' and extreme anxiety, which sets the scene for a range of behavioural responses. These responses can be seen as an attempt to mediate emotional arousal and exert some control over the physical and social environment, over which they often have very little control (Clements, 2005; Grandin, 1984). There is a risk that these behaviours and responses may be seen as just 'part of the condition' rather than attempts to communicate about distress.

Provisional and incomplete lists of threat reactions, described in terms of activated responses not 'symptoms' and running in a rough spectrum from pre-reflective to reflective, can be seen in Box 4, with further examples of threat responses in Boxes 5–8.

Box 4: Threat responses

Preparing to 'fight' or attack

Preparing to 'flee', escape, seek safety

Freeze response

Hypervigilance, startle responses, insomnia

Panic, phobias

Fragmented memory encoding

Memory suppression (amnesia)

Hearing voices

Dissociating (losing track of time/place; various degrees of splitting of awareness)

Depersonalisation, derealisation

Flashbacks

Nightmares

NEAD ('non-epileptic attack disorder')

Emotional numbing, flattening, indifference

Bodily numbing

Submitting, appeasing

Giving up, 'learned helplessness', low mood

Protesting, weeping, clinging

Suspicious thoughts

Emotional regression, withdrawal

'High' or extreme moods; rapid mood changes ('emotional dysregulation')

Holding unusual beliefs

Having unusual visual, olfactory, tactile sensations

Physical sensations – tension, dizziness, physical pain, tinnitus, sensations of heat or cold, exhaustion, skin irritation, gastrointestinal problems and many other bodily reactions

Emotional defences: denying what has happened, idealising people, and so on.

Intellectualisation (avoiding feelings and bodily sensations)

Attention/concentration problems

Confused/unstable self-image/sense of self

Confused/confusing speech and communication

Self-injury of various types

Self-neglect

Dieting, self-starvation

Bingeing, over-eating

Self-silencing

Mourning, grieving

Self-blame and self-punishment

Body hatred

Compulsive thoughts

Carrying out rituals and other 'safety behaviours'

Collecting, hoarding

Avoidance of/compulsive use of sexuality

Impulsivity

Anger, rage

Aggression and violence

Suicidal thinking and actions

Distrust of others

Feeling entitled

Reduced empathy

Distrust

Avoiding threat triggers

Striving, perfectionism, 'drive' response

Using drugs, alcohol, smoking

Overworking, over-exercising, etc.

Giving up hope/loss of faith in the world

Relational strategies: rejection and maintaining emotional distance; seeking care and attachments; taking on caring roles; isolation/ avoidance of others; dominance, seeking control over others; and so on

Ruminating, reflecting, anticipating, imagining, interpreting, meaning-making

Box 5: Examples of threat responses more common in children and young people

Eating/sleeping problems

Poor concentration, distractability

Impulsivity

Bed-wetting

Nervous tics, skin picking, etc.

Stealing

Speech and developmental delay

Bullying others

Running away from home

Hitting, biting

Extreme fear of separation

Phobias

Cruelty to animals

Emotional withdrawl, regression, rocking

Truanting

Poor peer relationships

Sexualised behaviour

Box 6: Examples of threat responses more common in people with intellectual disabilities

'Self-injurous behaviour': skin-picking, eye-gouging, head-banging, pica

Other 'challenging behaviours' that may be attempts at communication, especially if expressive abilities are limited, such as hitting, biting

Box 7: Examples of threat responses more common in older adults with cognitive impairments

'Wandering', searching for familiar places

Repetitive' behaviour or questions

Persistent shouting or screaming

Agitation, restlessness

Verbal or physical aggression

Hiding or hoarding objects

Emotional lability

Disinhibition

Box 8: Examples of threat responses more common in people with a range of neurological impairments

Anxiety

Insomnia, fatigue

Concentration and attention problems

Low mood

Emotional lability

Disinhibition

Provisional General Patterns

The discussion above now brings us to the point of being able to illustrate how the 'building blocks' within the elements of Power, Threat, Meaning and Threat Response, can be loosely grouped together to form Provisional General Patterns within the Foundational Pattern. These patterns are not presented as a definitive and complete set; rather, they offer a starting point for further research and development. In line with the earlier discussion, they do not conform to a single, straightforward definition of 'pattern'; however, they do represent meaningful research-based associations, and are based on evidence relating to general human functioning, cause and effect links and underlying processes. The relevant bodies of theory and research have been extensively reviewed in the main publication and are summarised in relation to each pattern in Appendix 1 in that document.

To repeat the core message from earlier discussions: the experience of adversity sets up highly complex, overlapping, meaning-based, cumulative and synergistic patterns in which causality is contingent and probabilistic. Adversities are often correlated, and the number of possible combinations of response is almost infinite, potentially creating variation from person to person, or within the same person over time, even in the face of similar circumstances. The discrete causal pathways implied by psychiatric diagnosis do not and cannot exist in relation to the responses of agentic, meaning-making human beings to their life struggles. Nevertheless, it is possible to outline some general regularities which emerge from embodied human responses to their social and cultural, material and discursive contexts, rather than from hypothesised biological malfunctions. As we have said, these causal regularities are here conceptualised as patterns of meaning-based threat responses to power. For all the reasons described, the understandings of individual or group experiences which draw on these patterns will always be provisional and open-ended.

Since this represents such a major shift from traditional diagnostic thinking, some central points are worth re-emphasising:

The General Patterns do not represent discrete clusters

The General Patterns describe regularities which cut across diagnostic groups and overlap with each other. There is no hard-and-fast boundary between one pattern and another, and nor could there be. Within the PTM Framework this does not present problems of 'fuzzy boundaries', 'co-morbidity' or 'disjunctive categories'. **Rather, it acknowledges the irreducible complexity of people's responses to their circumstances,** the many meanings that the experience of adversities may generate, and the creative range of strategies that may be employed, at various levels of reflective awareness, to survive them.

The General Patterns are not one-to-one replacements for diagnostic clusters

Some of the General Patterns have rough correspondences to existing diagnostic categories – for example, the second one captures some people who attract the diagnosis 'borderline personality disorder', the fourth pattern does the same for some people who are diagnosed with 'schizophrenia', the fifth corresponds to some diagnoses of 'depression', and the sixth describes some people who end up in the criminal justice system with a diagnosis of 'antisocial personality disorder'. This is because psychiatric diagnoses do, to a very limited extent, reflect common psychosocial response patterns, albeit described in medical terms. **However, as the PTM patterns are based on functions not on 'symptoms', it is not possible to predict which pattern or combination of patterns might best describe the experiences of a person who has been assigned any specific diagnosis.** Equally, each pattern may describe people who have been assigned any one(s) of a range of psychiatric diagnoses, and some who have never been diagnosed at all.

The General Patterns do not offer universal explanations of specific types of 'symptom' or threat response

Each General Pattern includes a range of possible threat responses such as hypervigilance, hearing voices, restricted eating, and so on, grouped in terms of the functions they are serving. Conversely, each type of threat response may appear within several different General Patterns, and may serve a range of different functions. **The patterns attempt to restore links between the meanings of the threats and the functions that the threat responses are serving, not between specific causal events (either biological or psychosocial) and specific psychological outcomes (whether described as 'symptom' or emotion/behaviour).** There can be no universal explanation for why people feel anxious or low in mood, or why they hoard possessions or carry out checking rituals, or why they fear that they are being persecuted and spied on, and so on.

Having said this, the threat responses in each pattern are not simply random or all-inclusive. Threat responses at a more pre-reflective level (e.g. hypervigilance) have the most obvious causal links to the original threats (e.g. physical danger.) Threat responses at a more reflective level will be shaped to a greater degree by social learning and social discourses, thus leading to greater variation across cultures. By elucidating the narratives and discourses that are most available within a particular culture, the General Patterns help to identify links between common meanings (e.g. 'It is my fault that I was sexually assaulted') and common functions (e.g. 'I will relieve my guilt by self-injury'). However, these links will always have a degree of provisionality, especially at an individual level.

The General Patterns cut across boundaries of 'normal' and 'abnormal'

The threat responses do not conform to traditional boundaries of what is considered 'normal' vs. 'pathological' – thus, for example, socially-valued attributes such as overwork can sometimes be seen as serving the same functions of self-punishment/avoidance of emotional pain as self-injury. Similarly, the functions of the threat responses cut across the usual service boundaries – thus, addictions and violent or offending behaviour can be seen as survival strategies which serve similar survival purposes to 'delusions' or 'hallucinations', as may over-eating, smoking, risky sexual behaviour, and so on.

There will be patterns within the General Patterns

Within the General Patterns, it may sometimes be useful to consider sub-patterns relating to specific events or circumstances such as domestic violence, rape, homelessness, etc. This is because these events and circumstances may, in a particular social context, be the subject of especially strong meanings and narratives. For example, the social discourse about women as bearing responsibility for sexual assault means that rape very often triggers strong meanings of shame and self-blame. Equally, the social discourse about men as strong and in control means that being the victim of physical violence is likely to trigger dominant meanings about humiliation. In both these examples, we can expect to see common responses which have the function of managing the impact of these dominant meanings; the woman may keep the rape secret and punish herself by self-injury, while the man may attempt to restore self-respect by counter-aggression. It may be very helpful for people who have experienced these adversities to be informed about these common reactions. **However, there is no universal meaning or unique response in relation to any given set of circumstances, either within or across cultures.** We therefore put forward the sub-patterns related to particular circumstances very tentatively, with a reminder that they overlap with others, and that the strongest regularities will be likely to emerge at a general level.

The General Patterns will always reflect and be shaped by the ideological meanings that apply within local social, political and cultural contexts.

It has been argued that **the expressions and experiences of distress within a given society in a given historical era will be likely, at some level, to reflect a mismatch (perceived or actual) with its values and expectations,** as conveyed through social discourses and ideological meanings. Thus, in modern industrialised societies we might expect common patterns of distress to centre around such themes as struggling to: achieve in line with accepted definitions of success; separate and individuate from one's family of origin in early adulthood; fit in with standards about body size, shape and weight; fulfil wage labour roles; meet normative gender expectations, including those relating to identity and sexual orientation; compete successfully for material goods; meet emotional and support needs within a nuclear family structure; reconcile the values and expectations of having a different culture of origin; bring up children to behave according to received standards; as a child, fit in with educational systems; as an older adult, cope with loneliness; as someone with intellectual or other disabilities, compete in the job market; and so on. Similarly, we might expect to find common patterns of distress relating to the core human needs which are most likely to be threatened by the negative impacts of industrialisation and neoliberalism, such as social exclusion, marginalisation and disconnection. Finally, in Euro-American cultures we might expect to see an increased risk of attracting a diagnosis as a response to experiences that challenge Western concepts of personhood – for example, 'irrational' or non-rational beliefs, unusual spiritual experiences, and experiences such as hearing voices which do not fit with the notion of a unitary self. All of these themes can be recognised in the General Patterns outlined below.

It is recognised that there will be other General Patterns that are more relevant to groups and societies which have a different worldview, albeit one that is increasingly being supplanted by globalisation. For this reason, the list includes some very tentative illustrative suggestions about the functions that some of the 'cultural syndromes' identified in *DSM* and *ICD* may perform when seen from a PTM perspective. The aim is to demonstrate the general principle that the core elements of Power, Threat, Meaning and Threat Response can be found in all groups and societies, although adaptations would be necessary. However, it is emphasised that there is no implication that the PTM Framework should be imposed or exported where it is not needed. Rather, **the intention is to convey a sense of respect for the numerous culturally-specific ways in which individual and community distress is expressed, experienced and healed in the UK and around the globe.**

People will vary in their 'fit' or match to these Provisional General Patterns

Each of the General Patterns describes a spectrum of adversities and responses. Depending on their own unique histories and circumstances, **people may find themselves at any point on the continuum, from mild and temporary discomfort to very severe struggles and disabling distress, at any given time and in any given situation.** Contrary to the implication of global deficit imparted by a 'mental illness' label, no one should be seen as unable to function at all times and in all situations. Equally, we will all inevitably experience extreme forms of distress at some time in our lives, whether we have been psychiatrically labelled or not. Sometimes the operation of power may appear in subtler and socially acceptable guises – for example, through unquestioned assumptions about how 'normal' people look, behave, feel, and relate to each other. It may then be harder to detect the roots of less 'severe' but common threat responses such as anxiety, panic attacks, and general low mood.

Some people will recognise themselves within a particular pattern or sub-pattern; others will find it helpful to draw on two or more patterns and sub-patterns. This is not a weakness of the patterns but an acknowledgement of the central role of meaning within and across all human responses to adversities, which means that it is impossible to make simple statements about the origins or functions of any given expression(s) of distress. **However, this recognition allows for reinstatement of the human attributes of meaning-making and agency that are excluded within a narrow diagnostic model.** These can be realised through the process of drawing on the General Patterns to develop personal narratives, as discussed in more detail at the end of the chapter.

There will be community versions of the General Patterns

The General Patterns are here conceived as applying mainly to individuals and families, since this is the most familiar lens through which distress is viewed within Euro-American cultures. However, **it is recognised that both within and beyond the UK, we might see patterns describing the traumatisation or denigration of a whole community as a more natural starting point.** This is particularly applicable within contexts of communities affected by war, natural disaster, or large-scale loss of culture, identity, heritage, land, language, rituals and belief systems (e.g. Jankovic et al., 2012; Somasundaram & Sivayokan, 2013; Steel et al., 2009). Trauma-informed work increasingly acknowledges the ways in which indigenous groups such as American Indians and Aboriginal peoples are affected by community violence on this scale (see Arthur et al., 2013, and www.preventioninstitute.org).

The community perspective has recently gained credibility in the US, with the recognition that Adverse Childhood Experiences arise within the contexts of Adverse Community Environments. Whole communities may be collectively impacted by structural violence, defined as 'harm that individuals, families and communities experience from the economic and social structure, social institutions, social relations of power, privilege and inequality and inequity' (Pinderhughes et al., 2015, p.11). These social contexts foster distrust and erode resilience at multiple levels, affecting all members both directly and indirectly, thus echoing and reinforcing individual patterns of distress (e.g. Rosen et al., 2017). Characteristic patterns of 'symptoms' of collective trauma may be experienced at the level of the social-cultural environment (the people), the physical/ built environment (the place) and the economic environment (the availability of resources and opportunities). It is suggested that this needs addressing at multiple levels, which include the development of a new and more hopeful narrative about the community itself (Pinderhughes et al., 2015). It is easy to see how this might apply to UK communities affected by conflict (e.g. Northern Ireland), by the loss of traditional industries and by high levels of deprivation. Such a view is also compatible with a social identity approach, which shows that an important part of our self-concept derives from perceived membership of social groups (Jetten et al., 2012). This is a possible area for further development of the patterns, perhaps utilising the framework suggested by the Adverse Community Environments research (see Pinderhughes et al., 2015) and/or by adapting part of the PTM Foundational Pattern.

The seven provisional General Patterns

The discussion up to this point has set the scene for outlining seven provisional General Patterns within the Foundational Power Threat Meaning pattern. The first General Pattern, 'Identities', is suggested as a useful starting point for everyone, since it is intended to highlight core issues relating to identity, diversity, intersectionality, marginalisation and cultural devaluing, and (where relevant) the ways in which the specific identity of 'mentally ill' may interact with meanings and experiences as a whole.

In keeping with the principle of 'actively engaging threat reactions for protection and survival' rather than 'passively suffering biological deficits', these General Patterns, with the exception of the first, are titled in verb form ('Surviving X threat' rather than 'Suffering from X deficit').

1. Identities
2. Surviving rejection, entrapment, and invalidation
3. Surviving disrupted attachments and adversities as a child/young person
4. Surviving separation and identity confusion
5. Surviving defeat, entrapment, disconnection and loss
6. Surviving social exclusion, shame, and coercive power
7. Surviving single threats

1. Provisional General Pattern: Identities

This General Pattern is conceptualised as informing and underpinning all the others, and as such can serve as a starting point in working with particular individuals or groups. As with all the General Patterns, the presence of fewer threats and exacerbating factors and more ameliorating and protective ones implies the need for fewer and less disabling threat responses.

Narrative summary of the General Pattern

The Power Threat Meaning Framework demonstrates that distress may be experienced by anyone, including those whose social status is more privileged. Everyone is impacted by the negative operation of power in one form or another, and no one is immune from social and relational adversities. Higher social status can bring exposure to its own characteristic negative operations of power. However, as a generalisation, some identities offer much greater compensatory power, status, control and access to social capital in the face of distress than others, along with more options for support, escape, protection, safety and healing. This is confirmed by the evidence about class, 'race' and gender gradients in mental health, criminal justice and other welfare systems.

This pattern in relation to emotional or psychological distress therefore often, but not always, describes someone whose identity, or aspects of whose identity, has subordinate or devalued status. This includes many people of minority status (for the purpose of this document, within the UK, although worldwide they may be a majority). It may also describe the experiences of a majority, and as such, may be an inescapable part of many people's everyday lives. In such cases the pattern may be even less visible than some of the other patterns and more accepted as culturally normal. The devalued identity may relate to ethnicity, nationality, sexual orientation, gender identity, religion, disability or being defined as 'mentally ill', but it may also relate to much larger groups who identify as female, older, or working-class.

As with all the patterns, occupying several marginalised identities (e.g. black and disabled; female and poor; gay and 'mentally ill') implies a greater degree of discrimination and threat, and increases the likelihood of experiencing other relational and social adversities, along with physical health problems. Conversely, and protectively, people may experience strong social solidarity within their group and/or have aspects of their identity that are more culturally valued.

As a general rule, all mental health diagnoses are more common in people with devalued identities, especially when they belong to several devalued groups. For example, people from minority ethnic backgrounds living in the UK have much higher rates of both common and severe diagnosed mental health problems than their white British counterparts. This holds whether they were born in the UK or moved to the UK from other parts of the world. It also holds for some white minority groups in the UK such as the Irish. Other marginalised groups, including women, Gypsies and travellers, people with disabilities, people identifying as gay, trans and disabled, and people of any background with low socio-economic status, are more likely to be diagnosed as having both common and severe mental health problems in proportion to their numbers.

Power, Threat, Meaning and Threat Responses within the General Pattern

The Power, Threat, Meaning and Threat Response aspects of this General Pattern commonly include the following:

Power

The person and their social group are likely to have past and ongoing experiences of multiple forms of subordination, exclusion and oppression related directly or indirectly to a devalued aspect of their identity, although this is not true for everyone. These may take the form of chronic background threats (such as living in deprived and unsafe environments or with frequent reminders of the potential for violence or aggression against your group), or of discrimination (in pay and employment, education, housing, transport, healthcare and so on). It may also take the form of numerous encounters with negative stereotypes of your group, of hostility and harassment and of 'micro-aggressions' or multiple, brief daily interactions which often subtly denigrate individuals in relation to their group membership. Harder to detect are potentially traumatic practices which are seen as socially acceptable or even desirable. Devaluing of a social or cultural group also extends to 'hermeneutical' or 'epistemic injustice', in which members are denied the opportunity to make sense of their own experiences due to unequal power relations and lack of shared social resources. All of this may occur in a context of historical and inter-generational oppression of a whole social or cultural group by, for example, warfare, colonialism or in extreme cases, genocide. The negative operation of ideological power may be especially salient given its role in the creation of meaning and identity, norms and standards against which group members' behaviour, character, skills and value may be judged. Ideological power is also closely related to 'hermeneutical injustice' (see above).

Threat

The person (and their family/social/cultural group) within this pattern was and is often faced with core threats resulting from the devaluing of core aspects of their self-concept and identity, including social exclusion and marginalisation within the dominant group, 'othering', physical danger, invalidation, powerlessness, competitive defeat, material deprivation, and loss of bodily integrity, as well as loss or devaluing of social role, community bonds, loss or devaluing of sources of knowledge and understanding, loss of rituals, practices or homeland.

Meaning

The threats are commonly associated with meanings such as: exclusion, shame, humiliation, entrapment, inferiority, worthlessness, powerlessness, and injustice/unfairness.

Threat Responses

The threats, and the meanings they are associated with, give rise to threat responses that are mediated by the body. Threat responses are conceived of as fundamentally protective. Disabling aspects can be minimised and counteracted by other responses which draw on skills, strengths, material, relational and social support, alternative narratives, and other power resources, many of which operate at the more 'reflexive' end of the spectrum, and may be more available to those occupying more privileged positions. In this pattern, such resources may take the form of social solidarity and awareness of ideological power, leading to social action. Since all of us occupy a range of identities, we may be able to draw on the

---

advantages offered by more privileged aspects. Threat responses within this pattern are commonly employed to serve the functions:

Regulating overwhelming feelings (e.g. 'high' mood, low mood, hearing voices, use of alcohol and drugs, somatic sensations, rage, bodily numbing, isolation, self-blame, self-injury).

Protection from physical danger (e.g. hypervigilance, fight/flight/freeze, suspicious thoughts, isolation, aggression).

Maintaining identity, self-image and self-esteem (e.g. denial of 'othering' or discrimination, hypervigilance, suspicion, unusual beliefs, perfectionism, aggression, striving).

Preserving a place within the social group (e.g. striving, competitiveness, appeasement, hypervigilance, suspicious thoughts, self-blame, self-silencing).

Protection against attachment loss, hurt and abandonment (rejection of others, distrust, seeking care and emotional responses, submission, self-blame, isolation, self-blame, appeasement, self-silencing).

Sub-patterns within the General Pattern 'Identities'

Since this General Pattern consists of a large number of often intersecting identities, there is no attempt to provide an exhaustive list of the implications for psychological and emotional distress in each case. Instead, indicative examples of distress in relation to a small subset of identities for which there is the most research evidence are suggested. Additional references providing a starting point for patterns of emotional distress in relation to these and other identities are provided in Appendix 1 of the main publication, along with detailed discussion of links between identities and distress. The intention here is to emphasise that core identities are relevant to the experience and expression of all kinds of distress and troubled or troubling behaviour, and to demonstrate that this awareness must inform the exploration of every individual or group response pattern to adversity.

A more detailed overview of the identity of 'mentally ill' is provided, since by definition it has been applied to, and taken on by, many people in distress or having unusual experiences.

Being identified/identifying as 'mentally ill'

Being ascribed the identity of 'mentally ill' or 'mental/psychiatric patient' is a very powerful act which has been shown to have profound, long-lasting and often negative impacts on many aspects of people's lives, including their psychological or emotional distress. This often includes their physical health, either through indirect effects such as poor diet and lack of access to healthcare, or through the direct effects of psychiatric medication. Since people whose identities are devalued are more likely to experience adversity and consequent distress, and thus be assigned psychiatric diagnoses, the addition of the devalued identity of 'mental patient' may increase and amplify existing experiences of shame, failure, exclusion and marginalisation.

The 'illness like any other' model of distress is actively promoted in high-income countries and, increasingly, across the globe, and is endorsed by a growing proportion of the general public. Worldwide, this view is associated with increased rather than reduced stigmatisation, and with social rejection and pessimism about recovery, along with self-stigma and self-blame. The diagnostically-based model of 'mental illness' can be seen as an aspect of the individualism that characterises Western cultures. The promotion of a model based on individual deficit has been argued to serve purposes at individual, social, professional, business and political levels.

The identity of 'mentally ill' has mixed consequences. It may represent relief from guilt and uncertainty, and hope for expert guidance and effective intervention. At the same time, the 'sick role' identity has been theorised as facilitating passivity and a reduced sense of responsibility for one's recovery. Diagnosis has been shown, overall, to incline the person diagnosed to have less optimism about recovery, make less effort to recover, and be more likely to use alcohol to cope, as well as to have lower perceived control over their difficulties and undermining the effects of therapy. Conversely, rejecting one's diagnosis has been linked to better outcomes. However, this may lead to conflict with professionals, and the need to access services and benefits rules out this option for most people.

Self-stigma as a consequence of being designated 'mentally ill' is very widely reported. People may have positive, negative or mixed reactions to being psychiatrically diagnosed, which may change over time. This depends partly on the diagnosis, and labels such as 'schizophrenia' which indicate greater 'severity' are generally experienced as more stigmatising. 'Personality disorder' labels are often reported as the most stigmatising of all due to the implication of a global judgement of madness and badness, and are also known to evoke, or be the consequence of, rejecting attitudes in staff. Diagnoses like 'depression' or 'anxiety disorder' are more likely to be perceived as helpful by service users, for reasons such as relief from guilt and self-blame, access to information and support, and validation of one's distress.

Psychiatric diagnosis has been shown to increase these aspects of the general public's attitudes towards people who have the identity of 'mentally ill': perceived dangerousness; perceived unpredictability; perceived dependency, and lack of responsibility for own actions; perceived lack of 'humanity'; perceived severity of the problem; fear; rejection and desire for distance; and pessimism about recovery.

Discrimination as a result of being designated 'mentally ill' is almost universally reported. This forms a barrier to employment and education, as well as everyday activities such as holidaying and leisure pursuits. These experiences are compounded for people from minority ethnic backgrounds and people with disabilities. Discrimination has a negative impact on seeking help, self-esteem, self-care and social relationships as well as being a source of guilt, shame and concern for family members/carers.

Psychiatric diagnoses facilitate access to important sources of support, both within and outside mental health services. Mental Health and related teams typically offer a range of interventions alongside standard medical ones, including various types of therapy, support with living skills, educational opportunities and building social networks, assessment for housing and employment, and so on. Some people have a good experience of services and find them very helpful. Most people report mixed experiences, both good and bad. On the negative side, psychiatric diagnosis can also set the scene for potentially disabling, coercive and re-traumatising interventions within mental health and related systems, including long-term use of medication, and compulsory admission, seclusion or restraint. The imposition of an expert narrative of 'illness' may undermine people's confidence and ability to make sense of their own experiences. More subtly, the identity of 'mentally ill' may limit people's expectations of who they can be, what they can achieve, and the kind of life they can hope to live.

Indicative examples of other well-established patterns in distress related to particular identities

Being identified/identifying as female

Girls and women make up around half of those who occupy other devalued identities. In many, if not most, societies, females are represented and treated as inferior or secondary, intellectually, economically and socially. There are variations on this, for example a woman of high social status may be treated as in some ways superior to a man of low social status; some female roles, such as motherhood, may also be highly valued. Overall, however, females as a group are subject to greater control over their bodies and activities than men, are often presented in objectified or sexualised ways, with a very high value placed on their appearance rather than their achievements, and are subject to high levels of harassment, micro-aggressions and violence from men. There are also in the minority in many positions of power and influence, for example in government, the law, industry, science and research. Their situation is complicated by their close, often biological relationships with men and by the taken for granted nature of social structures, practices and relationships in which women's assumed inferiority is embedded and enacted. There is extensive evidence of the negative impact of all of this on women's and girls' mental health across a wide range of presentations including anxiety, low mood, 'psychosis', dissociation, sexual problems, sleep problems, post-traumatic stress, eating problems and self-injury.

Being identified/identifying as male

Although 'male' is not generally a devalued identity, the privileges associated with it often involve strict boundaries on positive aspects of this identity and devaluing of aspects which challenge these boundaries, especially behaviour and emotional expressions seen as closer to 'femaleness'. Men who occupy other devalued identities, for example in terms of socio-economic background or ethnicity will face particular problems in maintaining socially valued aspects of masculinity. All of this, in combination with the threats described in the other provisional general patterns, is reflected in high rates of suicide, violence to others, problematic drug and alcohol use as well as problems with anxiety and low mood.

Being identified/identifying as a member of a minority ethnic group (in the UK)

People from many minority ethnic backgrounds living in the UK have much higher rates of both common and severe diagnosed mental health problems. This holds whether they were born in the UK or moved to the UK from other parts of the world, and has been shown to be related to experiences and perceptions of discrimination and racism, along with numerous other forms of social disadvantage. There are intersections with social class and gender. Specific communities (Turkish, Polish, Romanian, Indian, Pakistani, Ugandan Asian, Somalian, Hungarian and so on) may face their own characteristic patterns of challenge (see Appendix 1 of the main publication, for indicative references). Irish people in the UK have a record as poor as, or worse than, many of the main minority ethnic groups living in England in terms of both 'mental health' and physical health, and this disadvantage persists into second and third generations.

Being identified/identifying as of African or African-Caribbean heritage (in the UK)

Black people are a minority group in the UK and like many other UK minority groups, face additional hardship and discrimination including being very under-represented in positions of power and influence. The impacts are partly mitigated by living in close proximity to other black people. Black people of African and African-Caribbean heritage living in the UK have particularly high rates of diagnoses of 'psychosis'. This has been shown to be related to generally higher levels of social disadvantage, including poverty, racism and discrimination. Young black men living in urban environments in the UK have especially high rates of diagnosed 'psychosis', including higher rates of 'paranoia', which may be attributable to living at the point where multiple forms of disadvantage and discrimination intersect. Historically, the association of 'schizophrenia' with black males and with violence, hostility and paranoia can be traced back to the Civil Rights Movement in the US in the 1960s, when this stereotype started to emerge. The 'illness' was previously thought to affect mainly white people and was associated with inability to function rather than violence. The stereotype has survived as shown by the fact that both the public and professionals are likely to over-estimate the likelihood of young black men being violent. Black men are more likely to be compulsorily admitted to psychiatric hospital and subject to other forms of coercive intervention. Urban environments raise the risk of distress for everyone, but particularly if there are large disparities of income. Living near greater numbers of members of your ethnic group is a protective factor. 'Paranoia' is associated with being male, low socioeconomic status, immigration, member of a minority ethnic group, and being a refugee. Studies have associated 'paranoia' with feelings including shame, anger, worthlessness, humiliation, entrapment, disconnection, powerlessness and injustice.

Black women living in the UK experience multiple adversities of ongoing racism, poverty and gender inequalities and report high rates of sexual violence and revictimisation. Sexual violence and victimisation are associated with severe depression and traumatisation. Stereotypes of black women's strength have been identified as barriers to black women receiving help from mental health and community services. Women report being offered medication but not access to counselling or therapy in mental health services.

Being identified/identifying as having an intellectual disability

Particularly those with 'mild' ID may experience shame and devaluating, and many seek to distance themselves from others with ID and support services, exacerbating feelings of isolation and 'difference'. Feelings of 'stupidity' are an everyday risk in negotiating the social world. Earlier research from the 1960–70s referred to attempts to 'pass as normal' e.g. 'The Cloak of Competence', at a high emotional cost to the individual. There may also be shame at having significant 'impairments' and experiencing discrimination in a highly individualised, achievement-oriented society, leading to feelings of failure, 'not good enough', damaged, etc. This group is also more likely than their peers to have childhood experiences of physical, sexual and emotional abuse and neglect, which may be even less acknowledged than in the non-disabled population.

Appendix 1 of the main publication gives indicative references for emotional and psychological distress in relation to these and aspects of other identities including Gypsy/ Traveller, Irish (in the UK), LGBTQ, Low socio-economic status, Disabled, and Older Adults.

2. Provisional General Pattern: Surviving rejection, entrapment, and invalidation

As with all the General Patterns, this describes a continuum, and the presence of fewer threats and exacerbating factors and more ameliorating and protective ones implies the need for fewer and less disabling threat responses.

Narrative summary of the General Pattern

Within the Power Threat Meaning Framework, this describes a broad pattern of relationship threats and threat responses which give rise to core meanings of rejection, entrapment and invalidation. A central survival dilemma is maintaining attachments and relationships versus distrust and fear of rejection, hurt or harm. These situations arise more frequently in power contexts of poverty, social inequality, unemployment, gender inequalities, and war. Common diagnoses are 'borderline personality disorder', 'bipolar disorder', 'dissociative disorder', 'major depressive disorder', 'PTSD', 'alcoholism', and 'psychosis', although not everyone who is assigned one of these diagnoses aligns with this pattern, and these diagnoses are also assigned within other patterns. Poor physical health may compound the person's difficulties. Sometimes there is a history of criminal offences. Like all the patterns, this one may also describe people who have never been formally diagnosed.

Social and cultural discourses about gender roles in shape the way in which the threats are experienced and expressed. In many Western cultures, women show a tendency to direct distress inwards and men to direct it outwards, although anger is common in both. Sometimes overt abuse is absent, but emotional neglect, invalidation, criticism and control in early relationships may have resulted in similar threat responses. In service settings, the pattern is most frequently identified in women. This may result from the pathologising of responses such as anger or making demands that are seen as less acceptable in women. It may also relate to the fact that expressing anger inwardly, in line with female socialisation in some cultures, is more likely to result in a mental health referral than expressing anger outwardly in the form of violence to others. Sexual abuse, a powerful synergistic ACE for women, is very common in the early lives of women who are described by this pattern. Sometimes there has been organised abuse. Male veterans of combat may show a slightly different subset of responses (see also sub-pattern 'Surviving Combat').

The pattern describes some women in the criminal justice system, who may self-harm and have unstable lives and relationships. Women in prison report high levels of childhood abuse, domestic violence, and rape. As a generalisation, women are more likely to turn anger inwards into self-harm, eating disorders etc and men are more likely to turn it outwards in violence towards others. Women may be using illegal drugs, shoplifting, be involved in prostitution, or, more rarely, committing more serious offences. Their male counterparts are, for reasons related to gender socialisation, more likely to fall into the General Pattern 'Surviving social exclusion, shame, and coercive power'.

Most people with complex histories of adversity also show threat responses (such as flashbacks) to single traumatic events, and thus experience aspects of the pattern of 'Surviving single threats' as well, particularly in relation to men (and women) exposed to combat. As children they are very likely to have fitted the description of the General Pattern 'Surviving disrupted attachments and adversities as a child'.

Power, Threat, Meaning and Threat Responses within the General Pattern

The Power, Threat, Meaning and Threat Response aspects of this General Pattern commonly include the following:

Power

There has often been prolonged interpersonal maltreatment, abuse, invalidation and neglect in situations of lack of control, dependence, isolation and entrapment. In these situations the person was/is helpless and powerless in the face of emotional and/or physical threat, while often being dependent on the perpetrators for survival. These situations may originate with carers who were not able to facilitate secure early relationships due to their own social, material and personal circumstances, and/or to protect children from exposure to significant abuses of power; and/or they may occur outside the family of origin and/or in adult life. There is likely to have been significant traumatisation and re-victimisation as an adult. Backgrounds include neglectful and/or abusive early relationships; prolonged bullying as a child; domestic violence; combat. Other backgrounds include being a prisoner of war; being a victim of trafficking; survivors of organised sexual abuse; survivors of cults.

Threat

Core threats are rejection, invalidation, abandonment, attachment loss, entrapment, emotional overwhelm/dysregulation, powerlessness, physical danger and bodily invasion, physical ill-health and depletion.

Meaning

The threats are commonly associated with meanings such as: lack of safety, fear, rejection and abandonment, shame, guilt, emptiness, badness and unworthiness, alienation, betrayal, hopelessness, helplessness, and meaninglessness.

Threat Responses

The threats, and the meanings they are associated with, give rise to threat responses that are mediated by the body. Threat responses are conceived of as fundamentally protective. Disabling aspects can be reduced and counteracted by other responses which draw on skills, strengths, material, relational and social support, alternative narratives, and other power resources, many of which operate at the more 'reflexive' end of the spectrum. In this pattern threat responses are often used to serve the following functions, listed in rough order of how commonly they are employed:

Regulating overwhelming feelings (e.g. through dissociation, amnesia, disrupted attention, de-realisation, emotional numbness, bodily numbness, hearing voices, drug and alcohol use, self-harm, impulsivity, somatic sensations, splitting and projection of feelings, rapid changes of mood, unusual beliefs, suicidality).

Protection against attachment loss, hurt and abandonment (e.g. dominance and seeking control, distrust, vigilance for rejection, rejection of others, isolation/avoidance of others, self-silencing, self-hatred, self-blame, appeasement, compliance).

Seeking attachments (e.g. through idealisation, appeasement, self-blame, seeking care) Maintaining a sense of control (e.g. anger, dominance, eating habits).

Protection from danger (e.g. hypervigilance, anger and rage, anxiety, suspicious thoughts).

Meeting emotional needs/self-soothing (e.g. using drugs and alcohol, seeking secure attachments, self-injury).

Preserving identity, self-image and self-esteem (e.g. sense of entitlement, projection).

Communication about distress, eliciting care (e.g. self-injury, anger).

Sub patterns within the General Pattern 'Surviving rejection, entrapment and invalidation'

Sub-patterns within the General Pattern can be seen in relation to the following specific circumstances, among others:

Surviving domestic abuse (women): Women who witness domestic abuse as a child are more likely to be victims of domestic abuse as adults. Additional power issues may be present in the form of financial dependence and lack of alternative housing or support. The constellation of threats and threat responses in women who have survived or who are living with domestic abuse includes anxiety, low mood, fear, guilt, shame, increased risk of suicide, and physical health problems. They may use a range of safety and survival strategies including appeasement, isolation, self-silencing, and using alcohol and drugs. Common meanings, reinforced by the perpetrator, are to do with self-blame and worthlessness. The situation may be perpetuated by realistic fears of retaliation, along with lack of money, social support or alternative accommodation, and sometimes lack of awareness on the part of health and welfare professionals. Less is known about patterns in male victims of domestic abuse, or about abuse within gay or transgender relationships. There may be overlap with 'Surviving defeat, entrapment and loss.'

Surviving as a refugee, asylum seeker, trafficked or displaced person: This group has experienced numerous past and present Power threats including war, torture, bereavement, persecution and legal battles, along with the loss of family, income, work, homeland, and culture. These pose threats to every aspect of one's relationships, material security and social and personal identity. Meanings include hopelessness, grief, loss, fear, mistrust, isolation, lack of safety, and powerlessness. This may lead to threat responses including low mood, anxiety, nightmares, flashbacks, hopelessness, drug and alcohol use, and hearing/seeing missing relatives. Common diagnoses are 'PTSD', 'depression' and 'psychosis', with the more 'severe' diagnoses being more likely in the face of multiple traumas. There is overlap with 'Surviving single threats' and with 'Surviving defeat, entrapment, disconnection and loss'.

Surviving intergenerational and historical trauma: Work with the families of Holocaust survivors has laid the foundation for an understanding of 'intergenerational trauma' which can affect third and subsequent generations of a family through the psychological and emotional impact of living with trauma survivors. A related concept is historical trauma, a cumulative emotional wounding across generations caused by a subjugating population, as in colonialism, genocide and slavery in which entire peoples or colonised groups suffer from loss of language, traditions, and other forms of deliberate destruction of their lives and cultures.

3. Provisional General Pattern: Surviving disrupted attachments and adversities as a child/young person

As with all the General Patterns, this describes a continuum, and the presence of fewer threats and exacerbating factors and more ameliorating and protective ones implies the need for fewer and less disabling threat responses.

Narrative summary of the General Pattern

Within a PTM Framework the pattern describes situations in which the child's early relationships and/or environments were compromised due to a complex mixture of power factors such as intergenerational histories of trauma and adversity, lack of material resources, social pressures and social isolation. A combination of non-violent (e.g. emotional abuse/ neglect) and violent (e.g. sexual/physical abuse) trauma may be the most damaging. In more extreme examples, children may be subjected to organised abuse, or they and their families may be refugees or living in a war zone. The pattern can be manifested as 'disorganised attachment', in which an attachment figure is also a source of threat. This is likely to lead to threat responses based on dissociation, 'the escape when there is no escape.' Social discourses about gender roles shape the way in which the threats are experienced and expressed, such that girls may be more likely to react with dissociation and boys with overactivity and inattentiveness. Common diagnoses include 'attachment disorder', 'ADHD', 'oppositional defiant disorder', 'depression', phobias, and 'anxiety disorders', although not everyone within these categories fits the pattern and these diagnoses are also assigned within other patterns. There may also be physical health symptoms and conditions. In older children, the pattern may overlap with 'Surviving separation and identity confusion' or 'Surviving exclusion and competitive defeat as a young person' and there may be a history of criminal offences. Like all the patterns, this one may also describe children and young people who have never been formally diagnosed. As adults, they may be described by any of the other patterns, including 'Surviving rejection, entrapment and invalidation'.

Power, Threat, Meaning and Threat Responses within the General Pattern

The Power, Threat, Meaning and Threat Response aspects of this General Pattern commonly include the following:

Power

These children or young people have frequently been exposed to several or multiple adversities, including neglect, sexual, physical and/or emotional abuse, witnessing domestic violence, bullying, separation from or loss of parental figures (sometimes through institutionalisation), and in some cases, ritual or organised abuse. More subtle impacts of power may operate through school, social and community environments, familial and social comparisons and expectations, and so on.

Threat

Core threats are physical danger, emotional overwhelm, entrapment, emotional neglect, powerlessness, loss of agency and control, abandonment, identity confusion, physical neglect and bodily invasion.

Meaning

The threats are commonly associated with meanings such as fear, shame, worthlessness, emotional emptiness, abandonment, betrayal, hopelessness, feeling controlled, entrapped and defeated.

Threat Responses

The threats, and the meanings they are associated with, give rise to threat responses that are mediated by the body. Threat responses are conceived of as fundamentally protective. Disabling aspects can be reduced and counteracted by other responses which draw on skills, strengths, material, relational and social support, alternative narratives, and other power resources, many of which operate at the more 'reflexive' end of the spectrum. In this pattern they are often used to serve the following functions, depending partly on developmental stage, and listed in rough order of how commonly they are employed:

Regulating overwhelming feelings (e.g. self-injury, emotional numbness, changes of mood, drug and alcohol use in older children, dissociation, hearing voices, unusual beliefs, somatic sensations, bodily numbness, head-banging, memory gaps, attention and concentration disruptions, reduced empathy, impulsivity, over-activity, de-realisation, anger and aggression).

Protection against attachment loss, hurt and abandonment (e.g. distrust, self-hatred, compliance, making demands, anger, poor peer relationships).

Seeking attachments (e.g. sexualised behaviour, dominance, appeasement and compliance).

Protection from danger (e.g. hypervigilance, anxiety, restlessness, attention and concentration disruption, insomnia, distrust, aggression, biting, phobias).

Meeting emotional needs, self-soothing (e.g. rocking, headbanging, skin-picking, self-injury, rituals).

Communication about distress, elicit care (e.g. self-injury, self-destructiveness, tantrums, aggression and rage, seeking attachments, low mood, somatic sensations).

Maintaining a sense of control (e.g. rage, bullying, aggression, eating problems).

Preserving identity, self-image and self-esteem (e.g. bullying, dominance).

Preserving a place within the social group (e.g. bullying, dominance, appeasement).

Depending on age, there are likely to be developmental impacts on speech, language and behaviour milestones as well as on physical health and development.

Sub-patterns within the General Pattern 'Surviving disrupted attachments and adversities as a child/young person'

Sub-patterns within the General Pattern can be seen in relation to the following specific circumstances, among others:

Surviving witnessing domestic abuse as a child/young person: These children may be particularly likely, especially if boys, to pass on violence (cruelty to animals, aggression and temper outbursts, delinquency, fighting, bullying, threatening, poor peer relationships, disrespect for women, domestic abuse as an adult). This may involve a process of 'identifying with the aggressor'. Alternatively they (mainly girls) may resort to compliance, withdrawal, and feel great responsibility for the abused parent, as shown in high levels of guilt, anxiety, and separation anxiety. Later, adolescents and adults may seek affection through risky and indiscriminate sexual behaviour. The worse the violence in the home, the more severely children are affected.

Surviving sexual abuse as a child/young person: Child sexual abuse can have multiple long-lasting effects in childhood and adulthood, depending partly on exacerbating and ameliorating factors. It is a powerful synergistic ACE for both boys and girls. Girls who have experienced sexual abuse experience more frequent low mood, self-harm, dissociation, cognitive difficulties, numbing, impulsivity, distrust and dissociation than their non-abused female peers, along with lack of friends and troubled sexual relationships in adolescence. The damage is generally more severe if the perpetrator is the biological father, if it involves genital contact, and if there is earlier onset, multiple perpetrators and violence. Child sexual abuse also makes 'hallucinations' more likely, implying a high degree of dissociation (the 'escape when there is no escape') although it is not a specific or unique predictor of such experiences.

Surviving bullying as a child/young person: Bullying can be understood at one level as a process of enforcing group norms within peer groups. In this, it reflects the norms of the school, the media and the wider social environment, so that children who are perceived as deviating from these norms through appearance, socio economic status, ability or disability, gender, sex and sexuality, culture, race and religion are more likely to be targets. Bullying cultures thus have their origins in social and cultural norms, and in a general lack of tolerance for difference. Bullies may also need help; children are more likely to bully others if they have experienced parental maltreatment, especially physical and sexual abuse, and have witnessed domestic violence.

Bullying appears to be particularly common in UK schools. It may include physical and verbal assaults and 'cyberbullying' via social media. While there is no 'typical' recipient of bullying, victims are more likely to belong to groups that are already disempowered and discriminated against in other ways due to their sexuality, ethnicity, or disability.

The impact of bullying is often under-recognised, but can include poor academic performance, low mood, reduced self-worth, anxiety, self-injury and suicide as well as somatic complaints such as headaches, insomnia, stomach aches, and bedwetting. There is also an increased risk of 'psychotic' experiences in adolescence, which may include hearing the voice of the bullies. Longer-term implications for adults, depending partly on exacerbating and ameliorating factors, range from low self-confidence and loneliness, to 'psychotic' experiences. Bullying is a causal factor across a number of forms of distress in adulthood (see also 'Surviving defeat, entrapment, disconnection and loss', and 'Surviving social exclusion, shame and coercive power').

Surviving invasive medical interventions as a child/young person: Children who have to undergo repeated, painful and invasive medical interventions may be traumatised, partly because there is some evidence that younger children have a 'moral' explanation for healthcare treatment and interpret medical professionals/parents as intentionally causing them pain as punishment for wrongdoing. The treatment may also involve a degree of 'entrapment' or restraint ('clinical holding') which, while unavoidable in some circumstances, may exacerbate psychological distress.

Non-Western pattern: *Surviving conflict in Northern Uganda as a young person:* Spirit possession is reported in many cultures worldwide, and is associated with a range of situations, presentations and meanings, some positive, some less so. It does not feature in *DSM*, but is subsumed under 'trance or possession disorders', a subcategory of 'dissociative disorder NOS' in *ICD-10*. It is sometimes seen as equivalent to the psychiatric concept of 'psychosis'. One version, 'cen', is found in Northern Uganda, where civil war has resulted in widespread brutality and the abduction and forced recruitment of children as soldiers. In this phenomenon, young people report that their identity has been taken over by the malevolent ghost of a dead person. 'Cen' has been found to be associated with high levels of war trauma and with abduction, and the spirit was often identified as someone the abductees had been forced to kill.

4. Provisional General Pattern: Surviving separation and identity confusion

As with all the General Patterns, this describes a continuum, and the presence of fewer threats and exacerbating factors and more ameliorating and protective ones implies the need for fewer and less disabling threat responses.

Narrative summary of the General Pattern

Within a PTM Framework, this describes a pattern that is characteristic of individualistic cultures with a tradition of separation from the nuclear family in late teens/twenties, along with high achievement expectations. A central survival dilemma (reflected in the discourses of the wider culture) is finding a balance between emotional dependence, which may be experienced as trappedness and loss of self, versus separation and individuation, which may be experienced as abandonment and fear of failure. This dilemma commonly becomes acute in teens/early adulthood. Families may be isolated from support and caregivers may be struggling with their own cultural and gender role expectations and/or trauma histories. This may contribute to carer attitudes of protection, control and/or criticism, along with confusing communication styles. Social discourses about independence, striving, hard work, competitiveness and achievement may add pressure to the young person. Identity crises may also occur at other significant life transition points, such as bereavements, job loss, leaving a relationship or reaching a certain age. Common diagnoses are 'psychosis', 'schizophrenia', 'anorexia', 'bulimia', and 'OCD', although not everyone with these diagnoses fits the pattern and these diagnoses are also assigned within other patterns. Poor physical health may compound the person's difficulties. For adolescents and young people, there may be overlap with 'Surviving disrupted attachments and adversities as a child/young person'. Like all the patterns, this one may also describe people who have never been formally diagnosed.

Power, Threat, Meaning and Threat Responses within the General Pattern

The Power, Threat, Meaning and Threat Response aspects of this General Pattern commonly include the following:

Power

There has been long-standing difficulty in achieving a balance between dependence and individuation, sometimes starting early in life. There may be a background of parental separation or loss, or of sexual abuse and other traumas. Families of origin may be isolated from support. Social discourses about achievement and independence add pressure to the young person, who may have developed very high expectations of themselves. Western ideals about women's, and increasingly men's, body shapes are transmitted and supported by the media, diet, fashion, magazine and other industries, and set the scene for problematic eating and over-exercising as an expression of distress. (In some countries – e.g. Ghana, Hong Kong and South Africa – control rather than body size may be the dominant theme in restricted eating.)

Threat

There are core threats to identity, sense of self and agency, including emotional invalidation. Other threats are abandonment, emotional neglect, rejection, social exclusion and isolation, bodily invasion, and competitive defeat.

Meaning

The threats are commonly associated with meanings such as: abandonment, rejection, worthlessness, shame and inferiority, feeling controlled, invaded, entrapped.

Threat Responses

The threats, and the meanings they are associated with, give rise to threat responses that are mediated by the body. Threat responses are conceived of as fundamentally protective. Disabling aspects can be reduced and counteracted by other responses which draw on skills, strengths, material, relational and social support, alternative narratives, and other power resources, many of which operate at the more 'reflexive' end of the spectrum. In this pattern they are often used to serve the following functions, listed in rough order of how commonly they are employed:

Protection against attachment loss, hurt and abandonment (e.g. through fear of separation; denial/projection of anger and sexuality; compliance; self-silencing; emotional regression; confused identity and boundaries; low mood; anxiety).

Preserving identity, self-image and self-esteem (e.g. through unusual beliefs; self-starvation; anger; rebellion; perfectionism).

Regulating overwhelming feelings (e.g. self-starvation, self-harm, bodily numbing, unusual beliefs, hearing voices, carrying out rituals).

Protection from danger (e.g. through hypervigilance, appeasement).

Maintaining a sense of control (e.g. through rituals and compulsions; self-starvation and bingeing; over exercise).

Seeking attachments (e.g. dependency; compliance).

Preserving a place within the social group (e.g. through perfectionism, striving).

Self-punishment (e.g. self-blame, body hatred, self-harm, low mood).

Communication about distress, elicit care (e.g. through unusual beliefs, hearing voices, confused communications; self-starvation, rituals, low mood).

Finding meaning and purpose (e.g. unusual beliefs, controlled eating).

Sub-patterns within the General Pattern 'Surviving separation and identity confusion'

Sub-patterns within the General Pattern can be seen in relation to the following specific circumstances, among others:

Surviving midlife transitions: Significant distress is sometimes experienced by women facing a change of role after their children have left home, or other aspects of midlife including the death of parents. A similar pattern is sometimes seen in men. In both cases, there may be a drive to fulfil needs that have been denied or set aside through the necessity of meeting social and gender expectations earlier in life. For example, women's sense of identity may have been subsumed by the demands of child-rearing, exacerbated by messages about emotional self-sacrifice and by other social and economic inequalities. Men may be more likely to feel depleted by workplace expectations and the limitations of male socialisation.

Surviving separation within migrant families: Young people from first generation migrant families may experience the dual pressures to individuate according to Western cultural norms as exemplified by their white peers, and to remain in close contact with their families in line with cultural expectations. They may also have to negotiate compromises about styles of dress, use of drugs and alcohol, sexual relationships and so on. This, along with increased likelihood of unemployment and other forms of discrimination, may partially account for reported higher rates of distress including 'psychosis' in some minority ethnic adolescent groups.

5. Provisional General Pattern: Surviving defeat, entrapment, disconnection and loss

As with all the General Patterns, this describes a continuum, and the presence of fewer threats and exacerbating factors and more ameliorating and protective ones implies the need for fewer and less disabling threat responses.

Narrative summary of the General Pattern

Within the PTM Framework, this describes a broad pattern of threats, both past and present, and threat responses which give rise to core meanings of defeat, entrapment, disconnection and loss. Some degree of sadness, misery, loneliness and anxiety is an unavoidable part of life. However, if current environments are sufficiently long-term, severe and inescapable (e.g. workplace conditions; isolation from one's community; controlling partners; physical health problems; poverty; refugee status), the impact may be profound and disabling, even in the absence of earlier or additional adversities and losses. This pattern of distress is more common in less powerful groups, e.g. female, low social class, older age group, minority ethnic, especially in the context of austerity, social inequality and social injustice. These groups are also the most likely to feel the adverse consequences of high unemployment, low wages, poor work conditions, etc. Social discourses about striving, hard work, achievement, competitiveness and success may add to a sense of shame and defeat if these strategies do not succeed. In conditions of austerity and inequality, populations as a whole may experience increased levels of humiliation and shame; fear and distrust; instability and insecurity; isolation and loneliness; feeling trapped and powerless. This applies whatever one's personal background and experience of other adversities. It also affects more affluent members of society even if they are protected from the material impacts.

If 'depression' and 'anxiety' are taken as synonyms for some people who fit this pattern, it is more likely to be identified in women. This may be linked this to the dual trap of lower-paid, less valued work coupled with bearing the main burden of child care. However, one power factor, unemployment, may have a bigger effect on men due to its stronger links with male identities as workers and providers. Social discourses about families, childrearing, women's roles as carers, men's roles as earners and so on feed into expectations, and also set the scene for self-blame if these expectations are not met. Common diagnoses are 'depression', 'clinical depression', 'major depressive disorder', 'anxiety', 'generalised anxiety disorder', 'panic disorder', 'agoraphobia', 'alcoholism'/drug dependency, 'OCD', 'hoarding', 'postnatal depression', 'bulimia', and 'prolonged grief disorder' or 'complicated grief' along with suicidal feelings, although not everyone within these categories fits the pattern and these diagnoses are also assigned within other patterns. Poor physical health or pain and disability may compound the person's difficulties. Like all the patterns, this one may also describe people who have never been formally diagnosed.

Power, Threat, Meaning and Threat Responses within the General Pattern

The Power, Threat, Meaning and Threat Response aspects of this General Pattern commonly include the following:

Power

Within a PTM Framework, this pattern describes people who are trapped in long-term situations of chronic interpersonal/environmental stress and/or social exclusion. This may include poverty, controlling or unsupportive relationships, social isolation, bereavement, refugee status, workplace stress, unemployment, pain and disability, or child-rearing with insufficient support. At a broader level, it may describe the general impact of surviving situations of social inequality and injustice and the consequent fragmenting of communities which affects all its members. There may be early histories of disrupted attachments and trauma including loss of a parent, physical and sexual abuse, domestic violence, bullying, criticism or neglect.

Threat

Core threats include entrapment, social exclusion, competitive defeat, loss, attachment loss, loss of agency, loss of access to resources, physical exhaustion and depletion.

Meaning

The threats are commonly associated with meanings such as: helplessness, entrapment, defeat, loneliness, exclusion, lack of trust, self-blame, shame, humiliation, inferiority, unworthiness, and hopelessness. Other meanings may be a sense of alienation, failure, injustice/unfairness.

Threat Responses

The threats, and the meanings they are associated with, give rise to threat responses that are mediated by the body. Threat responses are conceived of as fundamentally protective. Disabling aspects can be reduced and counteracted by other responses which draw on skills, strengths, material, relational and social support, alternative narratives, and other power resources, many of which operate at the more 'reflexive' end of the spectrum. In this pattern they are often used to serve the following functions, listed in rough order of how commonly they are employed:

Protection against attachment loss, hurt and abandonment (e.g. appeasement, compliance, self-silencing, isolating oneself, dependence, 'giving up', exhaustion).

Regulating overwhelming feelings (e.g. withdrawal, avoidance ('agoraphobia'), low mood as a mask for grief, anger and loss, rituals, overwork, depersonalisation).

Self-punishment (e.g. low mood, self-blame, self-harm, suicide attempts, anger).

Maintaining identity, self-image and self-esteem (e.g. striving, competitiveness, self-starvation, perfectionism, body hatred).

Preserving a place within the social group (e.g. appeasement, compliance, dependence, striving, competitiveness, body hatred).

Seeking attachments (e.g. helplessness, weeping).

Meeting emotional needs, self-soothing (e.g. over eating, drug and alcohol use, exhaustion).

Protection from physical danger (e.g. anxiety, panic, phobias, withdrawal, 'agoraphobia', insomnia).

Maintaining a sense of control (e.g. rituals, rumination).

Communication about distress, eliciting care (e.g. self-injury, exhaustion, weeping, helplessness).

Sub-patterns within the General Pattern 'Surviving defeat, entrapment, disconnection and loss'

Sub-patterns within the General Pattern can be seen in relation to the following specific circumstances, among others:

Surviving competitive defeat: Some people demonstrate outward success through a strong achievement and competitive drive, derived from family and social expectations. If perceived expectations are not met, or it is not possible to sustain the drive, or they are suddenly faced with unemployment or other crises beyond their control, there may be threat responses of 'competitive defeat', exhaustion and self-criticism with a sense of failure, shame and hopelessness, and suicidal feelings. These reactions are likely to be more widespread within the general pressures of economic downturn and/or austerity, which have been shown to lead to generally increased levels of humiliation and shame; fear and distrust; instability and insecurity; isolation and loneliness; feeling trapped and powerless. Men may be more vulnerable to these messages and are the most at risk group for suicide. Within this, economically disadvantaged men in mid-life have the highest suicide rates. This may be due to a combination of factors including perceived failure to live up to masculine standards of success and control, in the context of relationship breakdown and socio-economic changes and pressures.

Surviving exclusion and competitive defeat as a young person: Adolescents and young adults in the UK report very high levels of self-harm, body hatred, eating distress, anxiety, misery, drug and alcohol use, etc., in the context of increased pressures to achieve in a more competitive environment, along with constant status comparisons through social media. The 'thin ideal' has resulted in an almost universal pre-occupation with weight in young women. Young men may have a parallel concern with being fit and having a well-defined physique. Austerity and inequality increase the pressures on everyone, and may impact strongly on young people through loss of opportunities coupled with social and economic pressures.

Surviving exclusion and competitive defeat as non-typical or non-conforming: The narrower the range of acceptable ways of being, and the more individualistic and competitive the social norms, the harder it is for people who are non-typical in various ways to find a social role and place for themselves and the more likely they are to experience feelings of failure, inadequacy, shame and exclusion. Some examples include: having an intellectual disability; having the characteristics associated with a diagnosis of Asperger's or autism spectrum disorder; being LGBTQ; having a visible appearance difference; and so on.

Coping with childbirth and childrearing: Sometimes diagnosed as 'post-natal depression'. Childbirth may involve aspects of threat such as entrapment, physical invasiveness, lack of control, loss of previous roles and status and so on, and for some women may re-trigger sexual/physical trauma memories. All of this may be exacerbated by hormonal changes, physical exhaustion, and so on. Longer-term power issues include lack of social support for families, isolated nuclear family structures, coupled with idealised messages about parenthood. Mothers, and sometimes fathers, who have received less than ideal parenting themselves, and/or have experienced earlier adversities and/or who are isolated and living in poverty, and/or are victims of domestic violence, are more likely to experience the emotional and physical demands of parenting as overwhelming and inescapable. Meanings are likely to include failure and entrapment. Threat responses serve the function of communicating a need for support and reparation, expression of unacceptable feelings, and escape, by means such as low mood, anxiety, intrusive images of harm, 'agoraphobia', self-blame and so on.

Surviving bullying and workplace bullying: Bullying can be understood at one level as a process of enforcing group norms within peer groups. Prolonged bullying in childhood is associated in adults with low mood and low self-worth, difficulties with trust and intimacy in romantic partnerships, shame and lack of confidence, and persistent loneliness. In its more severe forms, it may result in 'psychotic' and other difficulties as an adult, as described under the General Pattern 'Surviving rejection, entrapment and invalidation'. Although adults are, other things being equal, better equipped to deal with bullying than children, workplace bullying is a situation of entrapment and invalidation that is associated with panic attacks, low mood, loss of self-esteem, hyperarousal, avoidance, and physical symptoms such as headaches, insomnia, digestive problems, skin complaints, nausea, and heart palpitations. Bullying is more frequent in business or institutional environments that are primarily based on competition and threat.

Non-Western patterns: *'Brain fag'* in West Africa may be an expression of similar stresses. It is mainly reported by male school and university students and others studying for further qualifications, especially around periods of intensive study, and comprises mental exhaustion, sensations of pain or burning in the head and neck, and blurred vision. The experiences appear to be related to an intense desire to succeed and improve the economic and social standing of oneself and one's family. These pressures arise in the context of rapid social change and globalisation, and create tensions with more traditional values and practices. 'Brain fag' is a diagnosis that appears to be declining in use, with more recently trained psychiatrists applying it relatively rarely in practice. It has also been argued that it is not a true 'culture-bound syndrome' but a notion transported from 19th-century Britain.

The Khwe community in South Africa describes a version of kufingisisa, a phenomenon translated as 'thinking too much' which is mentioned in *DSM-5* and recognised in a number of world regions. While this state does not always have negative impacts or connotations for the Khwe, it sometimes refers to intense rumination about the extreme poverty, material deprivation and health concerns faced by this displaced and marginalised community. This is accompanied by feelings of hopelessness and lack of control.

6. Provisional General Pattern: Surviving social exclusion, shame and coercive power

As with all the General Patterns, this describes a continuum, and the presence of fewer threats and exacerbating factors and more ameliorating and protective ones implies the need for fewer and less disabling threat responses.

Narrative summary of the General Pattern

Within the PTM Framework, this describes someone whose family of origin is likely to have lived in environments characterised by threat, discrimination, material deprivation and social exclusion. This may have included absent fathers, institutional care and/ or homelessness. Within this, caregivers are likely to have been struggling with their own histories of adversity, past and present, often by using drugs and alcohol. As a result of all this, the person's early attachments were often disrupted and insecure, and they may have experienced significant adversities as a child and as an adult, including physical and sexual abuse, bullying, witnessing domestic violence, and harsh or humiliating parenting styles. 'Disorganised' attachment styles are common. Individuals tend to use survival strategies of cutting off from their own and others' emotions, maintaining emotional distance, and remaining highly alert to threat. Social discourses and status comparisons may have imparted a sense of worthlessness, shame and injustice, which may be managed by various forms of violent behaviour. More unequal societies, in which economic inequality increases social competition, allow these dynamics to flourish. This may have a particularly strong impact on disadvantaged men, who have greater incentives than women to compete, achieve and maintain high social status, while being faced with numerous indications of their lack of success and status.

'Paranoia', or suspicious thoughts, is very characteristic of this pattern (although not inevitably, and it is also found in other patterns.) It has been shown to have roots in disrupted attachments, domestic violence in family of origin, poverty, institutional care, unsafe urban environments, and experiences of bullying, assault and other physical threats. Minority ethnic status increases the likelihood of experiences of discrimination and exclusion, which may explain the greater incidence of suspicious thoughts ('paranoia') in these groups. 'Paranoia' can thus be seen as a possible response to exclusion and disconnection. Threat responses may include fearfulness, hypervigilance, appeasement, avoidance and self-isolation.

Violence and aggression have been shown to arise from similar roots as 'paranoia.' The two are sometimes, though not always, linked in this pattern, in that threat responses in the form of aggression may be very easily triggered in response to 'paranoia' or perceived danger, especially since the development of reflective abilities may not have been facilitated in early life. Gender socialisation means that men are more likely to direct anger outwards in the form of violence and destructiveness towards others, whereas women have higher rates of self-harm and eating distress. Women with these backgrounds may therefore be more likely to fit the pattern 'Surviving rejection, entrapment and invalidation'. The poverty that is a frequent feature of this pattern is a particularly strong synergistic ACE for both men and women.

While the PTM framework sees people as able to make choices in their lives, at the same time it acknowledges that these choices are often constrained. Thus, many (though not all) examples of violent and offending behaviour can be understood as survival responses. The pattern is therefore characteristic of a large number of males (and some females) in the criminal justice system (as well as of many people outside it). It has also been argued that 'anti-social personality disorder' is an extreme version of Western cultural stereotypes about dominant men with limited ability to empathise or express emotions.

Common diagnoses for men who are described by this pattern are 'antisocial personality disorder' or 'paranoia', while women are more likely to be diagnosed with 'borderline personality disorder', 'eating disorders', 'bipolar disorder' or 'major depressive disorder'. Another possible diagnosis is 'substance use disorder', although not everyone assigned these diagnoses fits the pattern and these diagnoses are also assigned within other patterns. Like all the patterns, this one may also describe people who have never been formally diagnosed.

Power, Threat, Meaning and Threat Responses within the General Pattern

The Power, Threat, Meaning and Threat Response aspects of this General Pattern commonly include the following:

Power

There have been multiple experiences of the negative operation of almost all forms of power giving rise to multiple social and relational threats and adversities, both past and present. This is commonly exacerbated by being sent to other threatening institutions such as prison. The wider context is one of competitive but economically and socially unequal societies, in which people, especially men, are faced with constant indications of failure and exclusion. Social discourses about gender roles shape the way in which the threats are experienced and expressed. This includes domestic violence, which is facilitated by discourses about male strength, dominance and control.

Threat

The individual (family/social group) within this pattern was and is faced with core threats such as social exclusion and disconnection, physical danger, emotional overwhelm/ dysregulation, emotional neglect and invalidation, humiliation, powerlessness, abandonment, material deprivation, and bodily invasion.

Meaning

The threats are commonly associated with meanings such as: fear, shame, humiliation, inferiority, worthlessness, and powerlessness, although there may be limited awareness and acknowledgement of this. Suspicious thoughts have been shown to arise out of feelings of powerlessness, injustice, shame, anger, entrapment, unworthiness and social exclusion. Fear of abandonment, emotional emptiness, emotional numbness, guilt and alienation may also be present.

Threat Responses

The threats, and the meanings they are associated with, give rise to threat responses that are mediated by the body. Threat responses are conceived of as fundamentally protective. Disabling aspects can be reduced and counteracted by other responses which draw on skills, strengths, material, relational and social support, alternative narratives, and other power resources, many of which operate at the more 'reflexive' end of the spectrum. In this pattern they are often used to serve the following functions, listed in rough order of how commonly they are employed:

Preserving identity, self-image and self-esteem (e.g. dominance, feeling entitled, violence, suspicious thoughts, sexual aggression, externalising, hypervigilance, distrust).

Regulating overwhelming feelings (e.g. denial, projection, reduced empathy and reduced awareness of emotions, suspicious thoughts, dissociation, numbness, somatic experiences, hearing voices, self-harm, drugs and alcohol, self-harm. Impulsivity, rage as a mask for fear, sadness, shame and loneliness).

Protection from physical danger (e.g. suspicious thoughts, distrust, dominance, aggression, hypervigilance, avoidance, self-isolation).

Maintaining a sense of control (e.g. maintain emotional and/or physical distance, use aggression as a defence against shame and humiliation, dominance, violence and threats).

Protection against attachment loss, hurt and abandonment (e.g. appeasement, maintain emotional distance, dominance, suspicious thoughts, violence, sexual aggression, sensitivity to humiliation and shaming, reduced empathy, impulsivity).

Preserving a place within the social group (e.g. aggression, gang membership).

Self-punishment (e.g. self-harm, suicide attempts).

Meeting emotional needs, self-soothing (e.g. drugs and alcohol, eating habits).

Sub-patterns within the General Pattern 'Surviving social exclusion, shame and coercive power'

Sub-patterns within the General Pattern can be seen in relation to the following specific circumstances, among others:

Perpetrating domestic abuse: Domestic abuse can refer to any violent or coercive relationship between adult family members, but most commonly it describes abuse between partners. Domestic abusers, like anyone who has committed a crime or behaved in a violent or coercive way, are accountable for their actions. At the same time, it is important to recognise that certain PTM patterns increase the likelihood that some people will choose to act in this way. Domestic violence perpetrated by men is more common in the presence of unemployment, lower socioeconomic status and financial stress. Early experiences of victimisation and witnessing parental domestic violence also increase the risk of this behaviour in men, but not in women. The level of exposure to violence in childhood is correlated with the severity of abuse inflicted as an adult. Domestic abuse is found in all sections of society, and some male domestic abusers have a profile of higher social status, and fewer or no other violent behaviours. Men described by this pattern sometimes attract diagnoses of 'narcissistic, antisocial or borderline personality disorders', and sometimes abuse alcohol. Less is known about domestic abuse perpetrated by women, although this may be linked to attachment disruptions and early trauma. Little is known about domestic abuse within same-sex and transgender relationships, although there are suggestions that insecure attachments and witnessing domestic violence may be relevant in gay and lesbian perpetrators as well.

Surviving homelessness: Long-term homeless people frequently report poor family relationships, high rates of emotional and physical abuse/violence including domestic violence, institutional care and substance misuse, in a cumulative series of adversities.

Surviving separation, institutionalisation and privilege: People from more affluent backgrounds may show somewhat different patterns of response. The earlier attachment disruptions, victimisation/trauma and the later threat responses may be more limited, subtle, and seen as socially acceptable or even desirable. Reduced empathy may be masked by social skills, superficial charm and high social status. For example, there has been description of so-called 'boarding school syndrome' among more privileged groups. The sudden loss of attachments at an early age, coupled with the need to survive in a new and possibly threatening or abusive environment, may lead to the development of a superficially confident presentation, which conceals vulnerability, fear and loneliness, even from the person themselves. This is likely to result in later difficulties with trust and intimacy, and (in the case of boys at single sex schools) relating to women. Sometimes, but certainly not always, this pattern is acted out in dominating, bullying or offending behaviour.

Non-Western sub-pattern: *Running amok* is a pattern of behaviour found in Malaysia and Indonesia among other places. It can take various forms, but in one, a hitherto peaceful man will acquire a weapon and make a frenzied attempt to injure or kill others. The episode frequently ends with the man either killing himself or being killed by others. Malay mythology attributed this behaviour to spirit invasion. It is also widely seen as a way to re-establish one's reputation as a man to be respected and feared, after a perceived slight. Comparisons have been drawn with school shootings in the US, which seem to be linked to male feelings of humiliation, rejection, failure, exclusion, grievance and anger.

7. Provisional General Pattern: Surviving single threats

As with all the General Patterns, this describes a continuum, and the presence of fewer threats and exacerbating factors and more ameliorating and protective ones implies the need for fewer and less disabling threat responses.

Narrative summary of the General Pattern

Within the PTM Framework, this pattern describes people who have experienced specific threat event(s), either directly or via witnessing harm to others. These may be non-intentional threats such as road traffic accidents, medical procedures, natural disasters, difficult childbirth, bereavement; or intentional such as rape, assault, torture, witnessing or perpetrating acts of war, and so on. The exacerbating factors apply, so that interpersonal and intentional traumas (rape, assault) are likely to have the greatest impact. In the absence of earlier adversity and attachment difficulties, the impact is, on average, less severe. Thus, specific threatening events such as sexual abuse, bullying, assault, difficult childbirth etc. may be survived without lasting distress given the absence of exacerbating factors and the presence of supportive and protective relationships. However there is likely to be at least some initial impact, mediated by the common social meanings of such events.

This pattern is widely recognised in Western settings under the diagnosis of 'PTSD'. The main differences within a PTM Framework are that the pathology implied by the term 'disorder' is avoided and aspects of social context are included. This allows for individual and cultural variation and recognises the centrality of meaning and function across all threat responses. It is important to note that the characteristic 'PTSD' criteria of hypervigilance, avoidance, intrusive thoughts and so on are not universal responses, either cross-culturally or historically (e.g. 'shell shock').

The pattern is also recognised in the trauma literature's distinction between 'single incident' trauma (an unexpected 'one-off' and 'out of the blue' event such as a natural disaster, traumatic accident, terrorist attack or single episode of assault, abuse or witnessing of it) and complex trauma which is cumulative, repetitive and interpersonally generated. Like all the patterns, this one may also describe people who have never been formally diagnosed. The more severe and long-lasting the threat(s), the more this pattern is likely to shade into other General Patterns such as 'Surviving rejection, entrapment, invalidation and adversities'.

Power, Threat, Meaning and Threat Responses within the General Pattern

The Power, Threat, Meaning and Threat Response aspects of this General Pattern commonly include the following:

Power

Power may be unrelated (e.g. bereavement from natural causes) or only indirectly related to single traumas. For example, a workplace accident may be caused by machinery, but the wider picture may be one of unsafe working conditions. A natural disaster may be outside human agency but its impact and aftermath (who was best protected? What aid was offered?) is likely to involve aspects of power.

Threat

The traumatic event was a threat to the psychological and/or physical integrity of the person and/or those close to them.

Meaning

The threats are commonly associated with meanings such as: fear, helplessness, isolation, alienation, self-blame, and shame. The last two are especially likely when traumatic events are experienced as highly personalised and intentional and when they are associated with negative cultural meanings. Threats that occur in the context of feelings of betrayal – for example, a war that is perceived as unjust or where others do not recognise the extent of trauma, or hold the person partly responsible – may have a more damaging impact.

Threat responses

The threats, and the meanings they are associated with, give rise to threat responses that are mediated by the body. Threat responses are conceived of as fundamentally protective. Disabling aspects can be reduced and counteracted by other responses which draw on skills, strengths, material, relational and social support, alternative narratives, and other power resources, many of which operate at the more 'reflexive' end of the spectrum. In this pattern they are often used to serve the following functions, listed in rough order of how commonly they are employed:

Regulating overwhelming feelings (e.g. avoiding triggers, drug and alcohol use).

Distraction from/avoidance of overwhelming feelings (e.g. drug and alcohol use, emotional and physical numbness, dissociation, memory gaps, depersonalisation, irritability, rage, self-silencing).

Protection from danger (e.g. fight/flight, hypervigilance, insomnia, rage, flashbacks, nightmares).

Maintaining a sense of control (e.g. hypervigilance).

Self-punishment (e.g. self-criticism, shame, guilt, low mood).

Meeting emotional needs, self-soothing (e.g. drug and alcohol use).

Sub-patterns within the General Pattern 'Surviving single threats'

Sub-patterns within the General Pattern can be seen in relation to the following specific circumstances, among others:

Surviving rape: Rape is known to have a more powerful impact than many other crimes due to its essential elements of terror, humiliation, powerlessness and bodily violation. Common threat responses and meanings include feelings of responsibility and hence self-blame, shame and guilt (especially in women) along with anger, relationship difficulties, and sexual difficulties. A similar pattern in men includes threat responses and meanings of humiliation, denial, repression, shame, powerlessness, low self-confidence, mistrust of adult men, sexual difficulties, negative body image and doubts about one's sexual orientation, along with internalised homophobia. Victims may be low in mood, anxious, fearful, panicky and/or suicidal in the aftermath of the assault, along with experiencing hypervigilance, avoidance, and intrusive thoughts, and may use alcohol or drugs to cope.

These meanings are shaped by social discourses about women's and men's roles, male and female sexuality and so on. Many rapes are committed by people known to the victim and may involve the perpetrator's minimisation or denial of what has happened – which in turn may be supported by wider social denial of what has happened. Victims who report the rape may encounter interpretations and legal processes which exacerbate their distress. Rape may also be used as a weapon against the civilian population in war, genocide and other forms of mass violence.

Surviving combat: These responses have long been recognised in forms such as 'shellshock' and were officially recognised with the inclusion of the new concept of 'Post-traumatic stress disorder' in *DSM-111*, following the Vietnam war. If threatening events in combat are characterised by many exacerbating factors, and occur in the context of a history of earlier adversities and attachment difficulties, the threat responses are likely to be more severe, and the pattern may be more typical of 'Surviving rejection, entrapment and invalidation.' It has been argued that the response patterns are essentially similar to those experienced predominantly by (mainly) women and children in the private sphere, as a consequence of rape, domestic violence and sexual abuse. War is particularly likely to expose combatants to extreme violence, violation, injury and grotesque forms of death, all of which are known to increase the likelihood of psychological damage to the witness. The survivor may remain in a state of physiological hyperarousal and preparation for threat, with accompanying insomnia, startle responses and irritability. They may experience vivid, fragmented and intrusive memories of combat events in the form of flashbacks and nightmares. They may attempt to manage all this by numbing their feelings and cutting off their perceptions, sometimes to the point of dissociating from their bodies. Drugs and alcohol may also be used to manage feelings of helplessness and terror. As with traumatic events in general, a sense of betrayal (for example, about the justification for war) increases the damaging impact by shattering the combatants' faith in themselves, other people and the world.

Non-Western pattern: *Surviving as a Cambodian refugee: Khyâl* attacks are reported in many Asian and South Asian countries, in which there is a belief in *Khyâl,* or a windlike substance that flows along with blood throughout the body. Bodily symptoms are frequently attributed to disruption of this flow. *Khyâl* attacks are characterised by palpitations, dizziness, shortness of breath, joint and neck soreness, tinnitus, headache, and loss of energy. The belief is that *khyâl* has suddenly started flowing up toward the heart, lungs, and neck. This causes the hands and feet to grow cold, while the upward flow of *khyâl* and blood potentially stops the heart or burst the neck vessels. The *khyâl* exits from ears or eyes, which causes the tinnitus or blurred vision. Cambodian refugees frequently report these attacks. In this group, the attacks are often related to reminders or memories of severe trauma experienced during the Pol Pot regime, including violence, death threats, and witnessing others being tortured or killed.

Part 5: Personal narratives within the Power Threat Meaning Framework

One of the main purposes of the General Patterns is to support the construction of narratives in their various versions, as an alternative to psychiatric diagnoses. 'Personal Narratives' in this sense can encompass individual, couple, family or social networks, depending on the situation and (if relevant) the model of intervention; and narratives may be of any kind, from structured psychological formulations to self-authored personal stories expressed in writing or any other medium. Since verbal or written narratives are the most common and often the most socially-valued form of expression in Western contexts, they are the main focus of this section, although other kinds of narratives (art, music, theatre, poetry, dance, and so on) are equally important and sometimes more helpful and relevant.

First, the issues pertaining to the contexts, forms, structures and functions of narratives, including the particular version that is known as formulation, are discussed.

Narratives – contexts and debates

Within the PTM Framework, the 'personal' meanings which constitute narratives are inseparable from the wider social discourses and ideological meanings from which they emerge. Chapters 2 and 3 of the main publication* offer an extensive discussion of the fact that '(a)ll societies have procedures whereby the production of discourses is controlled to preserve the structure and convention of that society (Hawtin & Moore, 1998, p.91). This connection between the personal and social/ideological works both ways. As Sherry Mead and Beth Filson observe, 'Through dialogue, new meaning evolves as we compare and contrast how we have come to know what we know. Our shared stories create communities of intentional healing and hope…When people share their stories without others imposing meanings on them, this creates social change' (Mead & Filson, 2016, p.109). The construction of a narrative through dialogue in this sense is, therefore, much more than an individual story. It is part of reversing the processes which, in the words of survivor Jasna Russo, 'devalue not only our personal stories but also our very ability to understand and make meaning of experiences of our own'. Instead, there is a need to '…take part in the production of official knowledge about madness and restore our own epistemic existence' (2016, pp.62–61).

It is important to remember that story-telling and meaning-making are universal human capacities, and as such there is an almost infinite number of additional examples of narrative and dialogical practices across the globe. Narratives at the level of the social group may be seen as equally or more valuable in collectivist cultures, where the idea of engaging in one-to-one therapy may be alien and inappropriate and there might consequently be more emphasis on locating emotional distress within the contexts of extended family relationships, ties to village and social network, relationship to house and

---

* Johnstone, L. & Boyle, M. with Cromby, J., Dillon, J., Harper, D., Kinderman, P., Longden, E., Pilgrim, D. & Read, J. (2018). *The Power Threat Meaning Framework: Towards the identification of patterns in emotional distress, unusual experiences and troubled or troubling behaviour, as an alternative to functional psychiatric diagnosis.* Leicester: British Psychological Society. Available from: www.bps.org.uk/PTM-Main

land, and so on (Bracken, 2002; Somasundaram & Sivayokan, 2013). For example, Davar and Lohokare's (2008) study of faith-based healing centres in India described how people's difficulties were 'woven into a larger narrative about life purpose, spiritual seeking, economic deprivation and social struggles' (quoted in Davar, 2016, p.15). Similarly, meanings may be more typically expressed as patterns within communities as a whole – both in terms of the damage that may have been done to the whole social fabric by war, natural disaster and so on, and in terms of supporting healing through shared community rituals and narratives. This damage is sometimes referred to as 'collective trauma', and as such, a collective response may be seen as more relevant (Somasundaram & Sivayokan, 2013). These perspectives are comparatively under-emphasised in more individualistic cultures, despite the strong evidence about the central importance of relationships and community ties for emotional wellbeing in all societies (Cromby et al., 2012).

The main publication discusses in detail how in Euro-American and Westernised cultures, experiences of distress are likely to be met by a powerful dominant narrative of medicalisation. However, as also discussed, narratives can be restorative and healing as well as limiting. This is a prominent theme in the lives of many former service users and in survivor-led movements. Thus, the emerging field of Mad Studies 'centres the knowledges of those deemed mad' in scholarship, theories, research and practice, as a way of resisting diagnostic and biomedical thinking (LeFrancois, 2016, p.v). Survivors/campaigners such as Jacqui Dillon and Rupert May concur that '… many accounts of recovery seem to be about a decolonising process' of 'reclaiming their experience in order to take back authorship of their own stories'. These new stories can transform discourses of deficit into ones of strength and survival, as part of 'our right to define ourselves; the right to find our own voices' (Dillon & May, 2003, p.16). This includes seeing your experiences as valid and meaningful; putting them in a wider context of social justice; joining together with others; and sometimes finding a new purpose that emerges out of suffering (Dillon & May, 2003, p.16).

It is important to acknowledge that distancing yourself from dominant expert narratives and constructing new ones, if that is your choice, is not a quick, easy or complete solution (Romme et al., 2009). This is partly because the discourse of medicalisation is so deeply embedded in our social institutions, theories, practices and everyday lives. It may be very hard to free oneself from the internalised stigma of diagnosis. Long-standing forms of distress may not disappear although it may be possible to find ways of living alongside them (as described in some of the early recovery literature). Healing from some of the consequences of diagnosis – such as the effects of medication – may take months or years, or perhaps never be complete. Struggles with finances, housing, low paid employment and so on may continue to dominate daily life. And caution is needed about co-option of the idea of narrative itself – as seen in pressure to produce an acceptable 'recovery story' while leaving basic diagnostic, economic and material structures unchanged. Critiquing this trend, Lucy Costa and co-authors (2012) note that 'It is now commonplace for mental health organisations to solicit personal stories from clients – typically, about their fall into and subsequent recovery from mental illness. These stories function to garner support from authority figures such as politicians and philanthropists, to build the organisational 'brand' regardless of programme quality, and to raise operating funds during times of economic constraint' (p.86). The authors warn that these 'sanitised' accounts, backed up by disclosures from well-known public figures, function 'to further solidify hegemonic accounts of mental illness' (p.87).

A similar cautionary note is needed about the growing trend for 'narrative based medicine' as a framework for a holistic, empathic understanding of a patient's physical illness and its meaning for him or her (Greenhalgh & Hurwitz, 1999). While this approach may have much to offer general medical practice, it cannot justify analogies between physical ill-health and 'mental illness' (see the main publication for discussion of the problematic 'parity of esteem' agenda). The medicalised 'illness' narrative is not simply another story that someone might be offered in relation to emotional distress or troubled/troubling behaviour, and its continued use by professionals raises questions of ethics as well as evidence.

Despite all the caveats above, there is still the possibility for approaches based on narrative, relational, dialogical and social justice principles to allow for what psychiatrist Judith Herman calls the 'restorative power of truth-telling' (Herman, 2001, p.181). This can provide a means for the person to locate their suffering within a wider social context, and replace exclusion and self-blame with a sense of compassion and community. In a jointly authored article, psychiatrist Philip Thomas and survivor Eleanor Longden concur that 'Just as the self can be undone and dehumanised by brutality and isolation it can be renewed and remade through solidarity and connection with others through narrative' (Thomas & Longden, 2013, p.4). These dialogues require, in Herman's words, 'a committed moral stance. The therapist...must affirm a position of solidarity with the victim. This does not mean a simplistic notion that the victim can do no wrong; rather, it involves an understanding of the fundamental injustice of the traumatic experience and the need for a resolution that restores some sense of justice' (Herman, 2001, p.135). There are obvious resonances with community psychology's emphasis on the core values of liberation, empowerment and social justice (Orford, 2008); with formulating within social inequalities and community psychology perspectives (Hagan & Smail 1997a, 1997b; McClelland, 2014); with the liberation psychologies of Latin America (Afuape & Hughes, 2016; Burton & Kagan, 2011); and with the process of 'conscientisation', or developing critical consciousness about the impact of societal structures on wellbeing, in which there is a shift from 'You are to blame for your circumstances and you must individually solve your problems with my expert help' to 'Certain social arrangements maintain particular groups in powerful and powerless positions, so let's act together to change them' (Nelson & Prilleltensky, 2010).

Using the Personal Narratives within the General Patterns

The PTM Framework is not intended to replace existing narrative and dialogical practices, or to re-package human abilities into professionally-owned skills. The longer-term aim is to make the PTM Framework an optional resource accessible to all. In the meantime, some initial thoughts about translating the PTM Framework into practice are offered below. Further resources, materials and good practice examples can be found in the Appendices.

The General Patterns provide a basis for developing personal narratives which fulfil more effectively the helpful functions of diagnosis as reported by service users, such as giving an explanation, having distress validated, facilitating contact with others in similar circumstances, offering relief from shame and guilt, and suggesting ways forward. A personal narrative drawing on the PTM Framework aims to promote understanding and influence/agency within the person/family/social network by: increasing awareness about the origins, both local and distal, of experiences of distress; identifying and demystifying the influence of social discourses and ideological meanings; restoring the links between meaning-based threats and functional threat responses; facilitating the relinquishing of narratives of stigma, shame and deficit; opening up alternative ways of living with/resolving emotional pain; increasing access to power and resources; increasing influence and agency within inevitable biological, psychological, social and material constraints and local cultural assumptions; and creating or co-creating a new and more hopeful narrative that supports and enables all the above. In narrative therapy evaluative terms, narratives informed by a PTM Framework are more likely to be 'thick' stories which increase influence and choice (Harper & Spellman, 2014). Appendix 1 suggests a template that may be useful in guiding this process.

As described earlier, Personal Narratives within a PTM or any other framework need to include two important additions to the information in the General Patterns (see Appendix 1). These are:

- The power resources available to the person and their social group, which moderate the negative impacts of power, convey a message of hope and resilience, and provide the basis for support and moving forward. In other words, we need to ask the question: 'What are your strengths?' (What access to Power resources do you have?)
- A summary of the evolving story, narrative, hypothesis or 'best guess' which integrates Power, Threat, Meaning and Threat Responses through the meanings they have to the person and their family/social network/community, and the strengths and resources that they can draw on. In other words, we need to work out 'What is your story?'

Clearly, power can be used in helpful (experienced as protective, enabling, supportive) as well as unhelpful (experienced as threatening, entrapping, invalidating) ways. Even the most disempowered individual/family and the most devastated community will have at least some access to sources of influence and resistance, which are more or less the opposite of the negative actions of power, as illustrated by Hagan and Smail's process of 'Powermapping' (Hagan & Smail 1997a, 1997b). These may encompass:

- Secure early relationships.
- Supportive current partners, family and friends.
- Social support and belonging.
- Access to material resources/cultural capital/education/ and so on.
- Access to information/alternative perspectives.
- Positive/socially valued aspects of identity.
- Skills/abilities – intelligence, resourcefulness, determination, talents.
- Bodily resources – appearance, strength, health.
- Belief systems – faiths, community values and so on.
- Community practices and rituals.
- Connections to the natural world.

This may enable individuals, families and groups to draw upon some of the following resources and strategies in response to threat:

- Regulating emotions by releasing/expressing/processing feelings (e.g. writing, exercise, talking therapies, body therapies, creativity and the arts, compassion-focused approaches, mindfulness, meditation).

- Self-care – e.g. nutrition, exercise, rest, alternative therapies.
- Using healing attachments/relationships for practical and emotional support, protection, witnessing, validation.
- Finding meaningful social roles and activities.
- Values and spiritual beliefs.
- Other culturally-supported rituals, ceremonies and interventions.
- Supporting each other in campaigning, activism.
- Creating/finding new narratives/meanings/beliefs/values/'survivor missions'.

Narrative use in current practice

There is already a rich range of narrative, dialogical and formulation-related practices to build on, each of which has characteristic strengths and limitations. Within services, this includes psychological formulations from various theoretical perspectives (Johnstone & Dallos, 2014; Corrie & Lane 2010); narrative therapy (e.g. White, 2000; and see Appendix 9); the Tidal Model (Barker & Buchanan-Barker, 2005); reflecting teams (Anderson, 1991); Open Dialogue (e.g. Seikkula & Arnkil, 2006; and see Appendix 10) and many others. Narrative approaches to emotional healing developed mainly outside services include the 'constructs' or personal understandings about voice-hearing from the Hearing Voices Network (Romme & Escher, 2000; and see Appendix 11); other resources developed by the Hearing Voices Network (e.g. The Maastricht interview); Intentional Peer Support, a form of peer storying and 'becoming part of each other's narratives' (Mead & Filson, 2016); the 'Tree of Life' approach initially developed in southern Africa (Ncube-Millo & Denborough, 2007) and now used in various settings including intellectual disabilities and young people (Denborough, 2008). Others have found art, poetry, painting, music, literature, sport, yoga and so on helpful in addition to, or instead of, counselling and therapy. Examples include the use of music technology to explore notions of masculinity with young offenders (Clemon, 2016); and film-making with young refugees and asylum-seekers (Clayton & Hughes, 2016). See also the Shared Voices and MAC-UK projects in Appendices 13 and 14.

Within this work, the concepts of testimony and witnessing may often be more relevant than those related to formal therapeutic intervention. Alec Grant (2015) has argued that all mental health professionals need to '...develop increasingly more sophisticated levels of narrative competence. .... This term refers to the capacity for human beings to deeply absorb, interpret, and appropriately respond to the stories of others. Such close attention facilitates methods for addressing users' existential issues around inner hurt, despair, hope....By carefully attending to context, nuance and difference within and between people's experiences of distress, narratively competent practice is helpful in engaging people who use mental health services in a recovery process through which they are able to re-story their lives' (Grant, 2015, p.52). This process of 'narrative re-storying' (Grant et al., 2015) is closer to the 'professional artistry' of reflective practice than to the dominant technical/rational model of medicine (Schon, 1987). The implication is that 'narrative competence' should inform every aspect of professionals' interactions with service users. This aligns with the principles of the Open Dialogue approach in which the shared dialogue is not a way of deciding on the intervention, but is itself the intervention and the means through which change can occur. Many service user/survivor accounts have illustrated the power of this process (Coleman, 2017; Grant et al., 2015; Longden, 2014; Romme et al., 2009; Waddingham, 2013).

The PTM Framework does not aim to supplant these existing practices, and clearly, the Personal Narrative template is not the only way of structuring a narrative, although it may have particular uses in some settings. Rather, the aim is to raise awareness about the aspects that existing narrative and formulation practices may under-emphasise. These are:

- The entrapping effect of the dominant narrative of psychiatric diagnosis and its wider context of meta-narratives about science.
- The contradictions inherent in combining psychiatric diagnostic narratives with psychosocial ones.
- The role of social discourses, especially those about gender, class, ethnicity and the medicalisation of mental distress, and how these discourses can support the imposition of others' meanings.
- The impacts of coercive, legal, and economic power.
- The nature and impact of power inequalities in psychiatric settings.
- The prevalence of abuse of interpersonal power within relationships.
- The role of ideological power as commonly expressed through dominant narratives and assumptions about individualism, achievement, personal responsibility, gender roles, and so on.
- The mediating role of biologically-based threat responses.
- The importance of function over 'symptom' or specific problem.
- The role of social learning and power resources in shaping threat responses.
- Culture-specific meanings, belief systems and forms of expression.
- Self-help and social action along with, or instead of, professional intervention.
- The importance of community narratives, values and spiritual beliefs, to support the healing and re-integration of the social group.
- Recognition of the varied, personal and provisional nature of all narratives and the need for sensitivity, artistry and respect in supporting their development and expression, whatever form they take.
- A meta message that is normalising, not pathologising (either medically or psychologically): 'You are experiencing an understandable and indeed adaptive reaction to threats and difficulties. Many others in the same circumstances have felt the same'.

The analysis presented in this and the main publication suggests that narratives of all kinds will be more holistic, helpful, healing, empowering and evidence-based if they draw on all aspects of the Power Threat Meaning Framework, as above.

Personal Narratives and Psychological Formulation

Psychological and psychotherapeutic formulations are one kind of narrative, and a narrative approach obviously has implications for the development of formulations.

Although training courses and some textbooks tend to describe formulation as if it is an event or 'thing', it is perhaps more accurate to see it as a process, an aspect of a shared exploration between two or more people, that has no definite end point. This is captured in the definition 'a process of ongoing collaborative sense-making' (Harper & Moss, 2003, p.8). The development of this personal story or narrative has been described as 'a way of summarising meanings, and of negotiating for shared ways of understanding and communicating about them' even though this can never be a final or 'true' account (Butler, 1998). In contrast to psychiatric diagnosis, psychological formulation approaches all expressions of distress with the assumption that '....at some level it all makes sense' (Butler, 1998, p.2). In other words, it represents a fundamentally different way of thinking about emotional distress, not just an additional activity or skill.

Psychological formulation as outlined in the Division of Clinical Psychology (DCP) (2011) *Good Practice Guidelines* already fulfils some of the criteria for narratives as listed above. Importantly, it is conceived of as an alternative to, not an addition to, psychiatric diagnosis: 'Best practice formulations...are not premised on psychiatric diagnosis. Rather, the experiences that may have led to a psychiatric diagnosis (low mood, unusual beliefs, etc.) are themselves formulated' (DCP, 2011, p.17). This is particularly relevant in mental health settings, although formulation is also used to provide a holistic understanding within Intellectual Disability, Older Adult, Neuropsychology and Health services, where a medical or neurodevelopmental condition will often be the main focus of intervention. The Guidelines recognise the damaging impacts of adversity, discrimination, deprivation and inequality (pp.14, 18, 20) and the potentially traumatising and re-traumatising role of services (p.20). It is recommended that psychological formulations include '...a critical awareness of the wider societal context within which formulation takes place' (p.20). It is noted that switching attention from individual deficits to 'injuries inflicted by a damaging environment...may...constitute a form of "demystification", bringing with it a significant degree of relief' (Hagan & Smail, 1997a, cited in DCP, 2011, p.20). There is recognition that psychological formulation itself is only one way of constructing narratives, and that it is influenced by Western assumptions about internal causation, individualism and self-actualisation (p.18). Finally, respect, collaboration and reflexivity are urged in the process of co-constructing formulations (p.30). Many of these principles are echoed in a core text from counselling psychology, Corrie and Lane's (2010) *Constructing stories, telling tales: A guide to formulation in applied psychology,* which emphasises the role of narrative and story-telling across the usual divisions of Psychology and the arts, and indeed in all human societies. The text offers helpful reflections about the definitions, uses, professional contexts, accuracy, evaluation and ownership of formulation.

The Personal Narrative template can be seen as another possible format for structuring psychological formulations with individuals, families and teams. More broadly, it is hoped that the PTM Framework will enrich the theory and practice of psychological formulation in whatever form it is currently used, and help to minimise some of the inherent risks of individualising, cultural insensitivity, imposing 'expert' views, and downplaying the causal role of adversities, both relational and social (DCP, 2011). This is an evolving field, and there are some interesting examples of formulating in relation to political and societal issues such as young people's 'sexting', debates about nuclear weapons, and the impact of legal processes on refugees (see *Clinical Psychology Forum* 2017, no. 293). Others are discussing ways of ensuring that formulations are culturally sensitive and appropriate (e.g. McInnis, 2017).

The DCP *Good Practice Guidelines* (2011) make an important distinction between psychiatric formulation – an addition to a psychiatric diagnosis – and psychological formulation – an alternative to a psychiatric diagnosis (p.17). It is probably not a coincidence that formulation, and debates about its role, have achieved growing prominence in the wake of the challenges to psychiatric diagnosis (e.g. Craddock & Mynors-Wallis, 2014). Now that formulation – in its psychiatric version – has become a core competency for all mental health and related professions (Skills for Health, 2016), extra vigilance is needed to promote, protect and develop those aspects of formulation and formulating that offer an alternative to medicalisation and psychiatric diagnosis.

Evaluating narratives and formulation

We have noted that the more variation across individuals and environments within the General Patterns, the more open, varying and provisional will be the personal narratives derived from them. We have also argued that this variation and overlap across the patterns is inevitable, since it arises from the highly contingent and synergistic nature of causality in human affairs, from the multiplicity, complexity and interacting nature of the factors involved, and from our roles as meaning makers and active agents in our lives. There can, therefore, never be one final, accurate and truthful account of the origins and meanings of someone's difficulties. Drawing from a psychoanalytic tradition, Stephen Frosh (2007) warns about the impossibility of ever reaching a final personal narrative that 'makes sense' because:

> *The human subject is **never** a whole, is always riven with partial drives, social discourses that frame available modes of experience, ways of being that are contradictory and reflect shifting allegiances of power as they play across the body and the mind (p.638).*

More generally, Bebe Speed (1999) has emphasised the combination of uncertainty and regularity which characterises personal narratives:

> *I can tell many stories about myself, who I am and the different selves or parts of me which are called forth in my interactions with others [but how] I behave and feel in any context is not random, but patterned. My life is not a fiction… Clients and I construct together some account of what's going on. It won't be the only one possible, the **truth** about the situation… There will be other versions of their situation that I (not to mention other therapists) and they together could have constructed that would also have had some fit and been relatively adequate to their situation (Speed, 1999, p.136).*

This raises an important question: In what sense, if any, can a narrative or formulation be said to be 'true', accurate, or in current terminology, 'evidence-based'?

The issue of evidence has been addressed more directly in relation to formulations, which differ from 'narratives' in a more general sense because they are defined by their explicit basis in established theory and bodies of evidence (DCP, 2011). Formulation-based practice is, in essence, a way of tailoring this evidence to the individual, with formulations serving as 'the lynchpin that holds theory and practice together' (Butler, 1998, p.2). In other words, 'formulations can best be understood as hypotheses to be tested' (Butler, 1998, p.2). Since developing and testing hypotheses is the heart of evidence-based practice (Sackett, 2002), it makes little sense to argue that formulations, either individually or as a whole, 'lack validity'. The validity of a particular formulation, or hypothesis, is tested out in practice and modified accordingly; and the strength of the formulation, or hypothesis, depends partly on the strength of the evidence it draws upon. This process will always involve a degree of uncertainty and provisionality.

In addition, in the case of both formulations and of narratives in general, we can reflect on how *useful* they are, from our different positions as professionals, service users, or simply people experiencing distress. Following Speed, we can think about how good a fit the new narratives have with actual lived experience, and the extent to which they enhance and enrich our lives or limit and diminish them – in other words, whether they 'make change conceivable and attainable' (Schafer, 1980, p.42) through providing a 'healing theory' (Meichenbaum, 1993, p.204). This usefulness depends on a different kind of 'truth', at least as experienced by the client, from that sought through 'evidence-based practice'. We are all familiar with the experience of suddenly reaching a new insight – whether through self-reflection, conversation, or a more formal process of therapy. This is illustrated by some client reactions to suggested formulations of their difficulties (Redhead et al., 2015):

> *'I think that sort of opened my eyes sort of, oh my goodness, that's what I'm doing. I really am doing that, and it's really not helping me. It's almost like algebra in school, it clicks all of a sudden' (p.459).*

> *'It all just made sense. I got it (the formulation), because it was true. It seemed true to me anyway' (p.459).*

Further experiential confirmation of the accuracy of a formulation came in the form of an emotional shift, and a sense of being able to move forward:

> *'My thoughts were all floating around at random, it was like a sort of storm inside my brain. But the diagram kind of took the pressure off. . .understanding it all was just like, phew, the storm was gone' (p.460).*

> *'I think if you know the reason something's happening, it automatically becomes more controllable. I could take control' (p.462).*

This was contrasted with the intuitive reaction to a formulation that did not feel true and was therefore not useful: (p.461).

> *'She was way off then, even suggesting it was down to my mum having a bad spell and me seeing her when she wasn't feeling good. And it was just like, no.' (p.461).*

In the case of both formulations and narratives, then, it is not enough to demonstrate that the theory underpinning them is sound, or that the facts of the person's life are historically accurate. It is possible for these requirements to be met and for the formulation to be experienced as unhelpful or inaccurate. One would hope that formulations grounded in established evidence would be more likely to bring about this experience of 'fit', but we cannot assume that this would be the case. Indeed, there is an opposite danger of shoehorning clients' experiences into a theory that is held too rigidly. People may also find elements of competing narratives useful, depending on the situation (Leeming et al., 2009). This is why client responses (which, ironically, are rarely considered in investigations into the validity of formulations; Johnstone, 2013) must be central to the evaluation of personal narratives and formulations.

The issue may become clearer by exploring Donald Spence's distinction between 'narrative truth' and 'historical truth'. He defines narrative truth as 'the criterion we use to decide when a certain experience has been captured to our satisfaction...that a given explanation carries conviction. Once a given construction has acquired narrative truth, it becomes just as real as any other truth' (Spence, 1982, p.31). In fact, he argues that, for the person concerned, narrative truth may have priority over historical truth 'because we are able to contain an unfinished piece of reality in a meaningful sentence' (p.137); in other words, to help someone to see things in a new way, which may help them to construct new meanings. These effects will be enhanced if interpretations have properties such as consistency, coherence and comprehensiveness. The notion of meaning is central here, because as Spence points out, psychotherapeutic work is based on theories about the meanings of situations and actions, not (as in the natural sciences) about more objectively verifiable events and processes. This is why the narratives constructed in therapy 'to an important extent...remain independent of facts' (p.292).

Formulations and related practices within therapeutic contexts can thus be seen as occupying a bridging position between narratives of science and narratives of subjectivity and personal meaning. While drawing on the established evidence-base, formulation also 'requires a kind of artistry that also involves intuition, flexibility and critical evaluation of one's experience...a balanced synthesis of the intuitive and rational cognitive systems' (Kuyken, 2006, p.30). This encourages us to adopt a more open and respectful attitude to non-clinical narratives – in other words, to the enormous range of stories that we may be presented with as clinicians, or that we may construct and live by as human beings. To give an example: elements of service users' narratives may be completely implausible, in terms of conventional evidence (for example, a belief that they are being tormented by the voice of the devil). In such situations, therapy often consists of a slow process of negotiating a different, less disabling narrative, which is equally unproven and unprovable – perhaps that the 'devil' is really a manifestation of unresolved abuse by a perpetrator who used the same words. Or perhaps the person may be able to draw on a different metaphor from within their own cultural belief system. In time, this new story may acquire narrative truth, and may thus help to open the person up to new ways of understanding and managing their distress.

What does the PTM Framework add to these complex issues? The argument is that it, along with the General Patterns that can be outlined by applying this lens, supports the claim that formulations and personal narratives informed by this perspective can be evidence-based. This applies in two important senses.

Firstly, as above, it has always been the case that best practice formulations are evidence-based in the sense of drawing on existing bodies of knowledge. The additional element that PTM supplies is a theoretical basis for grouping embodied, meaning-based threat responses into General Patterns. These higher-level patterns, underpinned by extensive theory and research, support the construction and content of specific formulations or hypotheses and put them on a firmer evidential footing. This 'clustering' is what psychiatric diagnosis claims, but fails to offer within its own terms – i.e. to provide support for the assumption that people with a certain diagnosis have something important in common, which derives from shared aetiology and suggests treatments targeted at known underlying dysfunctions. By abandoning the search for the kind of biological patterns needed to support medical diagnosis in favour of the very different approach needed to understand human behaviour and experience, we have been able to provisionally identify broad, meaning-based regularities which can serve a parallel purpose for formulations, but which draw on very different concepts of causality and shared aetiology.

Secondly, since the General Patterns are primarily organised around meanings – personal, social and cultural – they can be used to identify common patterns of meaning that may underpin particular narratives, whether those narratives are presented formally as formulations, or whether they arise informally as individual, family or group stories. Thus the PTM Framework's evidence about meaning-based patterns can help us to locate personal narratives within broader cultural meanings and discourses, and to identify and support the construction, where necessary, of more helpful and empowering ones which make sense within the person's own belief systems and which are likely to be experienced as having 'fit.' This may be supported by an existing evidence base, but we are also free to work (as the Hearing Voices Network www.hearing-voices.org and National Paranoia Network http://www.nationalparanoianetwork.org do) within any frame of reference that is meaningful to the person, in the knowledge that a mismatch with historical and scientific facts is not a barrier to constructing new and liberating narrative 'truths'. The PTM Framework thus has the potential to make narratives and formulations more evidence-based, in both the conventional sense and in the sense of facilitating the construction of 'narrative truth'.

What language do we use instead of diagnostic terms?

The question of language, especially in relation to everyday usages, is perhaps the most fundamental and important next step which underpins all attempts to develop alternative ways of understanding and responding to emotional distress and troubled or troubling behaviour. Alternatives for the purposes of service commissioning, research, access to benefits and so on are described in more detail in Chapter 8 of the main publication.

Changing our language goes much further than exchanging one disputed or stigmatising term for another. Rather, it implies replacing the whole discourse about what is called 'mental health'. 'Discourse' refers to organised and often unquestioned ways of speaking and using language which shape and transmit knowledge and the practices that depend on it (Foucault, 1979; 1980). Discourse is never used in a vacuum but always depends for its comprehensibility on other usually unarticulated statements which 'carry deeply entrenched convictions and explanatory schemas fundamental to the dominant form of making sense of the world in any given period' (Sawicki, 1991, p.104). Thus, changing language is not simply about using alternative vocabulary, but opens up new ways of thinking, experiencing and acting. Until this happens, we will simply continue to reproduce existing practices in slightly different, but equally unsatisfactory, forms.

It is for these reasons that there have been various attempts to outline alternative language uses, from both professional (DCP, 2014b) and service user/survivor (Wallcraft & Michealson, 2001) perspectives. Trauma-informed guidelines have similarly suggested a shift from 'symptom' to 'adaptation', 'disorder' to 'response' and so on (Arthur et al., 2013, p.24). BPS publications *Understanding bipolar disorder* and *Understanding psychosis* have acknowledged the debate and encouraged service user choice of terminology (BPS, 2010; 2014). However, this is a complex issue, with no single answer. Instead, we suggest a range of non-medical terms and phrases which may be suitable for different purposes and circumstances. In other words, instead of a 'new dogma' we need 'sensitive diversity in language' (Beresford et al., 2016, p.27). At the same time, we recognise that medicalised language will not change overnight; that developing new language uses is an evolving process that can only happen in tandem with a general shift in thinking about distress; that existing terminology will still be used – and therefore need to be used by others – for some current practical purposes such as access to services, or finding relevant literature and self-help groups; and that some people will continue to find diagnostic terms a useful shorthand description of their problems on a day-to-day basis.

Most importantly, we support individuals' right to make their own choice of terminology. At present, this right typically works one-way only: those who want their difficulties defined in diagnostic terms are unlikely to be denied this. The corresponding right, to refuse psychiatric labels, or even to be informed about debates and limitations, is rarely if ever offered. In fact, in many mental health, criminal justice and other welfare settings it may be unwise and unsafe for service users to reject their diagnosis in favour of alternative understandings.

At the same time as affirming people's right to describe their difficulties as they wish, we affirm the equally important principle that professionals, researchers, trainers, lecturers, charities, policy-makers and others involved in the mental health field should use language and concepts that have some claim to be descriptively accurate and evidence-based. Because psychiatric diagnosis does not meet these standards, it follows that it can no longer be considered professionally, scientifically or ethically justifiable to present psychiatric diagnoses as if they were valid statements about people and their difficulties. To draw an analogy from psychiatric history, once it becomes clear that terms like 'wandering womb' are mistaken, no professional should be offering – let alone imposing – them. The demise of current categories has been predicted by senior UK psychiatrists such as Paul Bebbington and Robin Murray; the latter has said he expects 'schizophrenia' to become as obsolete as 'dropsy' (2017). Existing terms will probably survive in ordinary language use for some time, since it takes a while for lay terminology to catch up, but these can no longer be professionally-sanctioned concepts.

However, it is not simply diagnostic terms which need to change. In order to think and act differently, the many language uses that imply, support and perpetuate the current model (patient, symptom, diagnosis, psychopathology, illness, disease, disorder, prognosis, remission and so on) also need to change. Three principles are suggested in the DCP *Guidelines on Language* for professional documents (DCP, 2014b): 1) Where possible, avoid the use of diagnostic language in relation to the functional psychiatric presentations (e.g. 'extreme mood swings' not 'bipolar disorder'; 'suspicious thoughts' not 'paranoia'). 2) Replace terms that assume a diagnostic or narrow biomedical perspective with psychological or ordinary language (e.g. 'problem' not 'symptom'; 'intervention' not 'treatment'). 3) In situations where the use of diagnostic and related terminology is difficult or impossible to avoid, indicate awareness of its problematic and contested nature (e.g. in an introductory note).

These principles can also be applied more generally. For example, researchers often use medicalised language such as illness, symptoms, and psychopathology unnecessarily. This not only continually reconstructs a problematic view of reality, it distracts attention from researchers' descriptions of what they are actually studying and risks losing valuable knowledge about people's experiences. This is not to suggest that researchers should not infer concepts or processes. The evidence presented here, however, suggests that these will be more valid if they reflect social contexts and relationships as well as individual behaviour and experiences. 'Dissociation', for example, refers to a functional, context-dependent process engaged in both by individuals and larger social groups.

It should be noted, however, that there is no entirely satisfactory substitute for terms like 'mental illness', 'mental disorder' or 'mental health', and the latter term has been unavoidable at some places in these documents. Nor will there ever be an adequate single replacement word or phrase, since the range of thoughts, feelings and actions that can lead to a psychiatric diagnosis encompasses almost every human experience, arises out of a complex multitude of contingent causal factors, and ultimately depends on local social and cultural judgements. One solution is to adopt a range of interchangeable, non-medical terms and use the one(s) which are the best fit for particular circumstances or usages. In this document we have alternated between emotional/psychological distress, problems, emotional difficulties, unusual experiences, and troubled or troubling behaviour. The DCP language guidelines suggest 'emotional distress, mental distress, severe mental distress, extreme state, psychological distress'.

As described in the main publication, access to services, benefits, housing and so on can be, and to some extent already is, determined on the basis of a professional endorsement that a person is experiencing severe psychological distress which impacts on daily functioning, or some synonym of this. For more specific purposes, non-medical problem descriptions such as 'hearing hostile voices' or 'suspicious thoughts' or 'very low mood' or 'feeling suicidal' or 'self-harming' can be a useful starting point for research and work within services, or as a basis on which to offer specific interventions, develop literature or set up support groups. Service design and commissioning can similarly be based on needs, specific population groups or problem categories rather than on diagnosis. Clustering terms such as 'complex trauma' are already used in some settings and pathways (Sweeney et al., 2016) and, even bearing in mind our cautions about the term 'trauma', are more relevant to people's actual problems and needs than current diagnostic groupings. Even if current systems demand that a diagnosis is recorded, *DSM-5* and the proposals for *ICD-11* allow for options such as 'Acute stress disorder', 'Adjustment disorder', 'Dissociative disorder' or 'Complex trauma' that acknowledge psychosocial rather than medical causes, and are on the whole less stigmatising than terms such as 'schizophrenia' which they may replace. Some computerised records allow space for a brief formulation-type summary – typically as well as diagnosis, but possibly instead of one in the future.

The issues in relation to everyday language use are also complex. One of the more difficult dilemmas for those who have been psychiatrically labelled is how to describe distress to others in a concise way that makes one's struggles seem reasonable and understandable. The many disadvantages of psychiatric diagnosis may be offset by their function of legitimising and (apparently) explaining distress to friends, family, employers and other lay people. As discussed by Leeming et al. (2009), narratives and formulations may seem to provide insufficient defence against attributions of shame or weakness, and because of the complex information they contain, are not appropriate for all purposes. The titles of the provisional General Patterns are probably not suitable for explaining distress to others, although adapted versions may be acceptable to some people (e.g. 'I am experiencing/struggling with/living with the effects of violence and neglect/abuse and trauma/loss and deprivation').

A balance may need to be found between verbs – more accurate, but also lengthier – and nouns. We have used the example of grief at various points. Because this is a universally-experienced form of distress, a phrase such as 'bereavement reaction' is generally understood to refer not to a disease or specific condition that someone 'has', but to a recognised emotional process, another way of saying 'I am grieving', Public education might help to bring us to the point where it is understood that phrases such as 'Trauma reaction', 'Separation difficulty', 'Attachment problems', 'Identity conflicts', 'Social exclusion' or 'Severe threat response' refer to similar processes of surviving the impact of life events and adversities. There should also be room for conceptualisations like 'Spiritual crisis'. Some service users want to reclaim the word 'madness', as in the 'Mad Pride' movement, while others definitely do not (Beresford et al., 2016).

These examples are not precisely-defined psychological (still less medical) concepts, but that is the point; as we have argued, patterns of human responses to adversity do not and cannot fall into neat categories. If we want shorthand ways of conveying the responses of people struggling with adversities, then these are better captured by 'fuzzy concepts' – in philosophical terms, categories that are open, inexact and yet still useful and meaningful in context, as many examples of everyday language are (Haack, 1996). Interestingly, the existence of lay versions of psychiatric language, such as 'stress' or 'nervous breakdown' suggests that general terms or fuzzy concepts like 'emotional/psychological crisis/breakdown' could serve as acceptable substitutes for the current pseudo-medical ones (Barke et al., 2000). It will no doubt be objected that these are not precise categories, but nor are the ones they replace. The crucial question is whether they are precise enough for their intended purposes. It is clear that they could be – and moreover, without the many disadvantages of diagnosis and the identity of 'mentally ill.'

A fundamental problem is the failure to find a midpoint between what has been called the 'brain or blame' dichotomy (Boyle, 2013). In other words, 'As a society, we seem to find it hard to find a middle ground between "You have a physical illness, and therefore your distress is real and no one is to blame for it" and "Your difficulties are imaginary and/or your or someone else's fault, and you ought to pull yourself together"' (Johnstone, 2014, p.2). Public health information about the limitations of current models is urgently needed. To return to what we said in the Introduction, the PTM Framework offers, instead, the resources to avoid this trap by constructing non-diagnostic, non-blaming, de-mystifying stories about strength and survival. In doing this, it opens up the possibility of replacing diagnosis with a range of ordinary language descriptions of these universal human experiences.

Conclusion

The ideas presented in this project are necessarily described mainly at a theoretical level, and much more work will be needed to translate the conceptual framework into practice. The project team welcomes feedback and suggestions for adaptation and improvement, acknowledging that at present the work is at an early stage of development.

The longer term aim is to make the PTM Framework into a publicly available resource, by developing accessible versions and materials to support professionals, carers, service user/survivors and anyone else who is experiencing/working with emotional distress. In the meantime, the Appendices give some examples of how non-diagnostic alternatives are already operating, together with suggestions and resources for further implementation of the ideas and principles in the Framework. In addition, Chapter 8 of the main publication gives a detailed overview and outline of the implications of the Framework in relation to: 1. Public health policy; 2. Mental health policy; 3. Service principles; 4. Service design, commissioning and outcomes; 5. Access to social care, housing and welfare benefits; 6. Therapeutic interventions; 7. The legal system; 8. Research.

Finally, it is important to emphasise these points:

- The core purpose of the PTM Framework is to outline a conceptual and intellectual resource that will take us beyond diagnostic and medicalised thinking and practice in relation to emotional distress, unusual experiences and troubled or troubling behaviour.

- The PTM Framework does not depend on any one theoretical orientation. Rather, it draws on general principles and evidence to present a fundamentally different perspective with the potential to enrich current theory and practice, as well as suggesting new ways forward.

- There can be no one-to-one replacements for existing psychiatric categories or terminology. The PTM Framework suggests a more fundamental shift in thinking which poses a challenge to all aspects of current diagnostically-based theory and practice, and applies across boundaries of 'normal' and 'abnormal'.

- The suggested General Patterns are provisional and incomplete and will inevitably change in response to further research and practice-based evidence

- A main aim of the PTM Framework is to restore the aspects that are marginalised and obscured by current diagnostically-based practice: the operation of power, the links between threats and threat responses, the wider social, political and cultural contexts; and the meaning-making and agency of those who are struggling to survive within their embodied personal, social, socio-economic and material environments.

- Narratives in the broadest sense can offer, and in many settings and cultures already do offer, a rich and meaningful alternative to psychiatric diagnosis. The PTM Framework suggests ways of supporting, conceptually, empirically and practically, the construction and co-construction of narratives, both within and beyond service settings.

Appendices

The Appendices have been compiled with the dual aim of demonstrating that non-diagnostic approaches are already being successfully implemented both within and outside statutory services; and suggesting ways to further integrate the ideas and principles underpinning the PTM Framework. As has already been noted, the PTM Framework itself is seen as a conceptual resource with the potential to inform a range of service, peer support, self-help, research, public engagement and policy initiatives.

Appendix 1 is a brief guide to how the PTM Framework could be used in direct client work, or in peer support or self-help contexts. It is designed as a basis for introducing people experiencing distress to the ideas underpinning the PTM Framework, and for allowing them to reflect on their own lives and experiences from this perspective. The material is not copyrighted, and the project team encourages people to use and adapt it as fits their own contexts.

The guided discussion in Appendix 1 includes a template. Existing templates which come from a similar perspective include Hagan and Smail's Powermapping (Hagan & Smail, 1997a, 1997b) and McClelland's 'Map of social inequalities' (McClelland, 2013). Hagan and Gregory (2001) have developed a version which supports groupwork with women survivors of sexual abuse.

Appendices 2–14 comprise a range of examples of work that is not based on diagnostic perspectives. The examples in 2–10 have been implemented within statutory services, and thus illustrate attempts to work alongside or modify and adapt existing systems. The examples in 11–14 have been developed outside services, and for that reason have had greater freedom to develop innovative non-medical approaches.

Type	Appendix no.	Title
Framework	1	A brief guide to using the PTM Framework to support narratives
Good practice examples	2	Complex trauma training for IAPT
	3	The Outcome-Oriented CAMHS model
	4	Team formulation
	5	Groupwork for women survivors of abuse
	6	Pathways in forensic work
	7	Trauma-informed pathways in AMH
	8	Formulation-based work in the Middle East
	9	Narrative approaches
	10	Open Dialogue
	11	The Hearing Voices Network
	12	Leeds survivor led crisis service
	13	Sharing Voices Bradford
	14	MAC–UK

Appendix 1

A brief guide to using the PTM Framework
to support narratives

These prompts and questions are adapted from the ones used with the project's service user consultation group. They are offered as a possible way to start reflection and discussion about how the PTM Framework might apply, in personal or peer supported use, or between service users and professionals. The same structure could be adapted for family or groupwork, or for staff training, consultation, supervision or team formulation. It is best used in conjunction with educational material about the impacts of various forms of threat on the mind, brain and body, such as http://cwmtaf.wales/services/mental-health/stabilisation-pack/. It may also be helpful to use the 'Identities' template (see end of this appendix) as a starting point. At the end, there is an option to compare the emerging story with the broader patterns described under 'Provisional General Patterns.' This may help to provide validation and reassurance, as well as placing stories in a wider societal context.

The prompts and questions below are very much open to development and adaption. The project team welcomes feedback, especially from those working in services such as Child and Adolescent or Intellectual Disability settings, where modifications will be needed.

The Power Threat Meaning Framework: Guided Discussion

'What has happened to you?' (How is **Power** operating in your life?)

'How did it affect you?' (What kind of **Threats** does this pose?)

'What sense did you make of it?' (What is the **Meaning** of these situations and experiences to you?)

'What did you have to do to survive?' (What kinds of **Threat Response** are you using?)

'What are your strengths?' (What access to **Power resources** do you have?)

'What is your story?' (How does all this fit together?)

Introduction to the discussion

The PTM Framework is an alternative way of understanding why people sometimes experience a whole range of forms of distress, confusion, fear and despair, from mild to severe. This is often called 'mental illness.' The PTM Framework is based on a great deal of evidence which suggests that if we know enough about people's relationships, social situations and life stories, and the struggles they have faced or are still facing, it is possible to make sense of these experiences. If we also think about people's strengths and supports, we may be able to come up with new ways forward.

Power Threat Meaning Framework Template

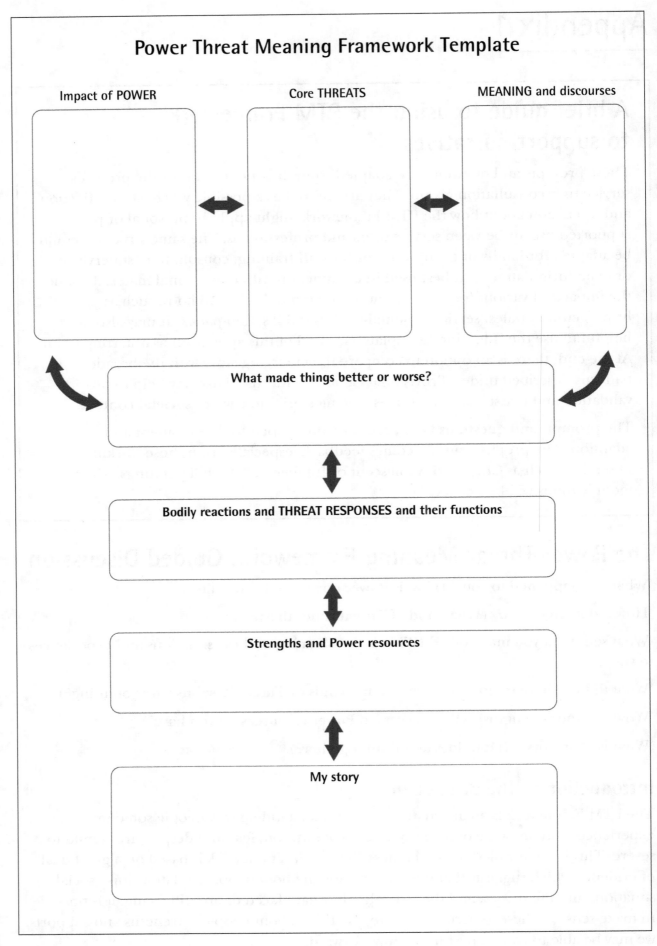

Figure 1: Power Threat Meaning Framework Template

The British Psychological Society, January 2018

The PTM Framework is based on the first four questions above. The fifth question is about skills, strengths and supports. The responses to all the questions can be summarised in the form of a personal narrative or story (sometimes called a 'formulation' in services.)

The prompt questions below are a starting point for reflecting, either on your own or with support from a friend, peer worker or professional, about how all of this may apply to you or your family/group/social network. Since the questions are closely related to each other, the responses may overlap. For example, talking about the way Power has influenced your life will be very likely to lead to naming some of the Threats that have resulted, and perhaps also some of the ways you have been affected by those threats and how you cope with them. It may be helpful to jot down these thoughts in the relevant boxes in the template below as you work through the prompts, rather than following the order of the questions too rigidly.

There is no right or wrong way to use the prompts and the template. Most people will need to take this process in stages. They may wish to come back to it and add in new thoughts and ideas over time.

The first part of the guided discussion invites you to think about the various ways in which power has affected you. The various types of power are described below. You may wish to jot down examples of how this may apply to you and your life.

POWER

'What has happened to you?' (How is Power operating in your life?)

'Power' can have several meanings. Generally it means being able to gain advantages or privileges, to arrange things to meet your own interests; or being able to gain advantages or privileges for others, to arrange things to meet their interests.

Power can operate through our partners, families, friends, communities, schools, work, health services, the police, government and the media. Power can be used negatively; for example when people are hurt, excluded or silenced by others. It can also be used positively, such as when others protect and care for us.

There is a great deal of evidence that the negative use of power, both in the past and in the present, can lead to mental health problems. There is also evidence that we can be helped and protected by positive and supportive power. Examples of the various kinds of power and the difficult events and circumstances that they can lead to, are given below. Some of them may apply to you.

Biological or embodied power is about our bodies and physical attributes. For example, we may enjoy strength, physical health, attractive appearance, sporting ability, and so on. On the other hand, we may experience physical limitations such as pain, disease, brain injury, disfigurement or disability.

Coercive power or power by force. Coercive power includes using aggression, violence or intimidation to make someone do things they don't want to do or to frighten or control them. Examples include being beaten as a child, bullying in school, domestic abuse, forced psychiatric interventions, or being mugged or attacked. On a wider scale, power by force happens in unsafe neighbourhoods, in systematic violence against certain groups of people, and in political conflict and war. Used positively, power by force can protect us from threats or dangers.

Legal power The law is needed so that we can all live in a fair and peaceful society where our rights are protected. The law is also used to prosecute or imprison people or otherwise restrict their freedom, in order to protect the rest of society. On the other hand, sectioning or coercion by Mental Health Law may be experienced as damaging, and sometimes the law fails to prosecute someone who has harmed you, or may not give equal rights to certain people or groups. The welfare system is backed by legal power so that people can get the benefits they are entitled to. However, the law can also be used to impose unfair or harmful policies on vulnerable people.

Economic and material power Having enough money to live on, with good housing and enough to eat, is essential to our wellbeing. It also makes it easier to escape or change things we are unhappy with, to protect our families, and to access help and support when we need it. Sometimes our financial security is at risk from others such as parents, partners, landlords, public officials, or employers, who may have control over your finances, income, housing and possessions. Welfare systems and wider social and economic policies and structures can also create and maintain poverty and inequality.

Social or cultural capital refers to whether or not we have access to socially valued educational, job training and leisure opportunities. It is also about whether we have, or know how to get, the knowledge and information we need to in order to live the life we want, and whether we benefit from social connections and a sense of social confidence and belonging in the society we live in. All of these benefits can be passed on to the next generation. Without them, we may feel we are excluded from or don't deserve various forms of influence and opportunity, such as jobs, education, healthcare and so on.

Interpersonal power – All of the other kinds of power can operate through relationships. In addition, our relationships offer important sources of security, support, protection, validation, love and connection. This helps to build a sense of identity about who we are, as individuals, and as members of families, social networks and wider communities. Relationships with others, including family, colleagues, teachers, friends, neighbours, employers, healthcare staff, and public officials can also have negative aspects such as neglect, bullying, abuse, abandonment, invalidation, shame, humiliation, discrimination and so on. These experiences can impact on us and our sense of ourselves and our identities very negatively, especially if they occur in childhood.

Ideological power This means power over meaning, language and 'agendas.' This is one of the least obvious but most important forms of power, because it is about our thoughts and beliefs. Ideological messages, or ways of looking at ourselves and the world, can come from a whole range of sources. Some examples are parents, social networks, schools, advertisements, healthcare staff, politicians and other public figures, as well as messages from the media, internet and social media. Whether these messages are positive or negative, they are extremely influential, and can feel very difficult to challenge, partly because they are often accepted as normal and unquestionable. Ideological power includes:

- Power to create beliefs or stereotypes about your group. Our sense of identity draws partly on various social identities – for example, as women, men, trans, black or minority ethnic, as an older person, as someone with mental health problems, or intellectual or physical disabilities and so on. We may also be identified as member of a sub-group, such as people who receive benefits, or lone parents. All these overlapping identities can have both positive and negative aspects.

- Power to tell people, directly or indirectly, how they should think, feel, look and behave in order to be an acceptable member of a group or of society. This can include almost anything, from the 'right' body size and appearance, to the 'right' lifestyle, the correct way to bring up children, express sexuality or religious beliefs, and so on. The further we are from fitting these standards, the harder it will be to develop a sense of confidence and self-worth.

- Power to silence or undermine you and/or your social group, for example through criticism, trivialising, undermining, deliberate misinterpretation of your views, intimidation, or sometimes by labelling you as 'mentally ill.' This can happen in direct contact with others, or indirectly through sources such as the legal system and the media.

- Power to interpret your experiences, behaviour and feelings and tell you what they mean. Ideally, children will be guided to develop their own understandings, beliefs and values. As adults, we may gain support from others who share our beliefs and worldviews. On the other hand, both children and adults can face silencing, invalidation, and having others' views and feelings imposed on them. Telling people that their experiences of distress are due to a 'mental illness', even if they disagree, can be seen as an example. This kind of power can work through many sources, including educational and social media material.

You will almost certainly have some ideas about how the various forms of power have affected you. The following prompts will help you reflect on this in more detail.

THREAT

'How did it affect you?' (What kind of Threats does this pose?)

When power is used in negative ways it often brings about very difficult and threatening situations or challenges. Some additional examples to help you think about threats in your own past or present life are given below.

Relationships: This can include parents, partners, other relatives, friends, colleagues, teachers, healthcare staff, and many others. As described above, relationship threats can include abandonment/rejection by or loss of loved ones or people you depend on; witnessing or experiencing domestic violence or bullying; being undermined or invalidated through criticism, hostility, humiliation, dismissing your feelings or beliefs; confusing communications; having other people's views or meanings imposed on you even if you don't agree with them; lack of love, care and protection; sexual, physical or emotional abuse; emotional, physical or material neglect; intergenerational trauma which is passed down through parents and other relatives.

Emotional: Faced with threats, people can feel unsafe and emotionally overwhelmed by a whole range of feelings which are very hard to manage.

Social/community: In their workplaces or local communities, people may face isolation, exclusion, hostility, bullying, sexual harassment, discrimination, loss of their social or work role, and so on.

Economic/material: This includes poverty, lack of housing, being unable to meet basic physical needs, or to access basic services for oneself and/or dependants.

Environmental: People may live, or have lived in, deprived and unsafe situations, either in their houses and/or in areas of poverty, conflict or war. They may have lost contact with their community, country of origin, and/or the natural world.

Bodily: This could include ill-health, chronic pain, disability, injury, brain injury, other losses of function, physical danger, starvation, exhaustion, having your body attacked or invaded.

Identity: This includes lack of support to develop your own beliefs, values and identity; loss of status; loss of social, cultural or religious identity, such as being a worker, a parent, or a member of a particular social or ethnic group. Without this, people and their social groups may be made to feel ashamed or devalued.

Value base: This includes loss of purpose, values, beliefs and meanings; loss of community histories, culture, rituals and practices.

Knowledge and meaning construction: Some kinds of ideological power may help to deprive people of the opportunity, support or social resources to question or make sense of their own experiences. For example, the internet gives access to huge amount of information, but this can also be manipulated to present certain viewpoints and suppress others. People's own knowledge, understanding and beliefs may be undermined due to unequal power relations between themselves and others. In the field of mental health, mainstream ideas and meanings may be promoted or imposed by family, healthcare staff, academics, media figures, researchers and others, making it hard to get information about alternative views on mental health. These situations may apply to large groups of people (e.g. women; the 'mentally ill'); or to certain individuals (e.g. by labelling them 'uneducated' or 'lacking insight').

Circumstances that make threats easier or harder to survive

These are some of the circumstances that are known to affect the impact of very difficult situations. You may have touched on them already in response to earlier prompts. These prompts may help you to think in more detail about the aspects of threat that were particularly hard for you, and also about some of the ways you managed to survive them.

- Whether you felt secure, protected and loved by your parents and carers during childhood.
- How old you were when any of these difficult events were happening.
- Whether the threat was a deliberate act by another person.
- Whether you felt betrayed or let down, by a person and/or an organisation.
- Whether you were faced with just one or several threats, and one or several perpetrators.
- Whether the threat happened once or was repeated or ongoing.
- How predictable the threat(s) were, and how much control you had over them.
- The severity of the threat(s) and whether or not there was any escape.
- Whether the threat was physically invasive.
- Whether the threats happened close together or at the same time.
- Whether the threat(s) were chronic and ongoing (environmental or personal).
- Whether there was a threat to your sense of self and who you are as a person.
- Whether the threat was from someone you were close to or depended on emotionally.
- Whether you had someone to confide in about the threats, who believed and protected you.

While thinking about threats, you will probably have been aware of the particular meanings that the threats had for you. For example, you may have felt afraid or ashamed. The following prompts will help you to reflect on this in more detail.

MEANINGS

'What sense did you make of it?' (What is the Meaning of these situations and experiences to you?)

Meanings in this sense include beliefs, feelings and bodily reactions. We all attach meanings to the things that happen to us. Often, but not always, we are well aware of these meanings. Sometimes the meanings tend to leave us feeling even worse – for example 'It was all my fault' or 'I am unlovable' or 'No one can be trusted' This is a list of meanings that are often relevant to people who have experienced threats. They may apply to you, at different times and in different situations. You might also want to think about positive meanings that have helped keep you going. For example, people in your past or present life may have helped you to feel loved, valued, and protected.

Box 1: Meanings

Unsafe, afraid, attacked	Trapped
Abandoned, rejected	Defeated
Helpless, powerless	Failed, inferior
Hopeless	Guilty, blameworthy, responsible
Invaded	Betrayed
Controlled	Shamed, humiliated
Emotionally overwhelmed	Sense of injustice/unfairness
Emotionally 'empty'	Sense of meaninglessness
Bad, unworthy	Contaminated, evil
Isolated, lonely	Alien, dangerous
Excluded, alienated	Different, 'abnormal'

Box 2: Threat Responses

Preparing to 'fight' or attack

Preparing to 'flee', escape, seek safety

Freeze response

Hypervigilance, startle responses, insomnia

Panic, phobias

Fragmented memory encoding

Memory suppression (amnesia)

Hearing voices

Dissociating (losing track of time/place; various degrees of splitting of awareness)

Depersonalisation, derealisation

Flashbacks

Nightmares

NEAD ('non-epileptic attack disorder')

Emotional numbing, flattening, indifference

Bodily numbing

Submitting, appeasing

Giving up, 'learned helplessness', low mood

Protesting, weeping, clinging

Suspicious thoughts

Emotional regression, withdrawal

'High' or extreme moods; rapid mood changes ('emotional dysregulation')

Holding unusual beliefs

Having unusual visual, olfactory, tactile sensations

Physical sensations – tension, dizziness, physical pain, tinnitus, sensations of heat or cold, exhaustion, skin irritation, gastrointestinal problems and many other bodily reactions

Emotional defences: denying what has happened, idealising people, and so on.

Intellectualisation (avoiding feelings and bodily sensations)

Attention/concentration problems

Confused/unstable self-image/sense of self

Confused/confusing speech and communication

Self-injury of various types

Self-neglect

Dieting, self-starvation

Bingeing, over-eating

Self-silencing

Mourning, grieving

Self-blame and self-punishment

Body hatred

Compulsive thoughts

Carrying out rituals and other 'safety behaviours'

Collecting, hoarding

Avoidance of/compulsive use of sexuality

Impulsivity

Anger, rage

Aggression and violence

Suicidal thinking and actions

Distrust of others

Feeling entitled

Reduced empathy

Distrust

Avoiding threat triggers

Striving, perfectionism, 'drive' response

Using drugs, alcohol, smoking

Overworking, over-exercising, etc.

Giving up hope/loss of faith in the world

Relational strategies: rejection and maintaining emotional distance; seeking care and attachments; taking on caring roles; isolation/avoidance of others; dominance, seeking control over others; and so on

Ruminating, reflecting, anticipating, imagining, interpreting, meaning-making

THREAT RESPONSES

'What did you have to do to survive?' (What kinds of Threat Response are you using?)

These ways of reacting to threat are sometimes called 'symptoms' but within this PTM Framework they are seen as 'threat responses'. They were necessary survival strategies when the threat(s) happened, and they may still be protective if the situation has not changed. In other words, they are there for a good reason. These reasons may include helping to manage overwhelming feelings; protection from physical danger; keeping a sense of control; protecting yourself from loss, hurt, rejection or abandonment; seeking or holding onto safe relationships; holding on to a sense of yourself and your identity; finding a place for yourself in social groups; meeting your emotional needs; communicating a need for care and help; and finding meaning and purpose in your life. However, some of these threat responses may no longer be needed or useful. In fact they may be causing you problems in their own right.

Threat responses lie on a spectrum from automatic bodily reactions, such as flashbacks or panic or the urge to fight or flee from danger, to more deliberate strategies, such as restricting your eating, or avoiding relationships, or using alcohol. Unusual experiences such as hearing voices or having mood swings or being overwhelmed by suspicious thoughts can also be seen as threat responses. The list in Box 2 may help you to identify some of your commonest or most troublesome reactions to threat.

(See Chapter 6 of the main publication for threat responses that may be more characteristic of children, older adults with cognitive impairments, people with intellectual disabilities, and people with neurological difficulties.)

STRENGTHS

'What are your strengths?' (What access to Power resources do you have?)

This may include people who care for you, aspects of your identity that you feel good about, skills and beliefs, and so on. Other possible strengths in your life, past and present, are:

- Loving and secure early relationships.
- Supportive partners, family and friends.
- Social support and a sense of belonging.
- Having the chance to enjoy material, leisure and educational opportunities.
- Having access to information/knowledge/alternative views (e.g. on mental health).
- Positive/socially valued aspects of your identity.
- Skills/abilities – such as intelligence, resourcefulness, determination, talents.

- Bodily resources – appearance, strength, health.
- Belief systems – faiths, community values and so on.
- Community practices and rituals.
- Connections to nature and the natural world.

You might want to think about some of these ways of building on your resources and strengths:

- Managing your emotions by releasing/expressing/processing feelings (e.g. writing, exercise, talking therapies, body therapies, creativity and the arts, compassion-focused approaches, mindfulness, meditation).
- Self-care – e.g. nutrition, exercise, rest, alternative therapies.
- Using or finding relationships for emotional support, protection, validation.
- Finding meaningful social roles and activities.
- Other cultural rituals, ceremonies and interventions.
- Getting involved in campaigning, activism.
- Creating/finding new narratives/meanings/beliefs/values.

What is your story?

When you have worked through all the prompts, it may be helpful to pull all this information together in the form of a narrative or story about your life, the difficulties you have faced, the effects all this has had on you, what it all meant to you, the ways you have coped, and the strengths that have enabled you to survive. The story is never final or complete and you will probably want to re-visit it.

Do other people have similar stories?

As well as offering a way to explore your own story, the PTM Framework summarises common patterns that can be found in many people's stories. These are called General Patterns, and they are based on a great deal of evidence about the impact of power, threat, meaning and threat response in people's lives. Sometimes it is helpful and reassuring to realise that other people have been through similar experiences and have reacted in similar ways. The General Patterns are described at www.bps.org.uk/PTM-Overview

It is important to note that:

- The General Patterns are not simple replacements for particular psychiatric diagnoses. They cut across diagnoses, and also include people with no diagnosis at all.
- Often there is no neat fit between a particular person and a particular General Pattern. Many people will recognise parts of their story in several patterns.
- The General Patterns are on a spectrum. The effects of power and threat on a particular person depends on many factors which make the impact either worse or better. Some people will have much milder difficulties, others will have greater struggles.
- The General Patterns will be amended and changed over time as more evidence emerges. In particular, we know less about typical patterns in non-Western cultures and settings, in the UK and across the world.

Identities

A person's sense of identity shapes every other aspect of their life and the way they respond to threats and difficulties. It may be helpful to think about how various aspects of your identity have influenced you. This is likely to include positive and supportive ways, such as feeling confident and being part of a group, as well as negative ways, such as being subjected to discrimination. You may wish to think about your ethnicity, class, age, gender, nationality, sexual orientation, religion, disability or being defined as 'mentally ill'.

The invented example in the diagram below describes a young, heterosexual woman from a working class background who has been involved in a serious accident which has left her partially disabled. She has overcome early disadvantage and built a successful career, but she is now signed off sick. She is having flashbacks to the accident, and is also coping with many changes to her life and ambitions. At the moment she feels trapped and hopeless about her future. She has taken part in a guided discussion about the PTM Framework and realises that her reactions are described by two of the General Patterns, 'Surviving defeat, entrapment, disconnection and loss' and 'Surviving single threats'.

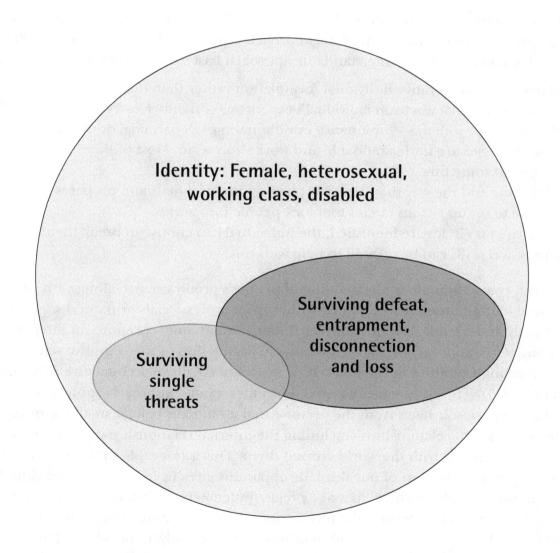

Identity: Female, heterosexual, working class, disabled

Surviving defeat, entrapment, disconnection and loss

Surviving single threats

Appendix 2

Complex Trauma Training for IAPT: 'Comprehend, Cope and Connect'

The Hampshire IAPT service, italk, conducted an audit of a patient cohort who had made limited recovery with the existing interventions, and identified them as having problems exacerbated by complex trauma. The Strategic Health Authority then funded a project to offer a tailored service for this group. 'Comprehend, Cope and Connect' (CCC), developed by Isabel Clarke (2015), was adopted as an approach that incorporates consideration of past trauma and relational aspects of therapy into its collaborative formulation and facilitates motivation towards clear treatment protocols for IAPT therapists. This is now being piloted in four sites across Hampshire, as a programme that links four individual, transdiagnostic, formulation sessions with an intensive 12 session group course, followed by one or two individual review sessions.

The CCC (formerly Emotion Focused Formulation or EFFA) model is described in Clarke (2008, 2009) and a pilot evaluation of the approach is published in Durrant et al. (2007). It is a flexible and intuitively understandable approach based on the following principles:

- It starts with collaborative individual formulation rather than diagnosis.
- It acknowledges that where an individual's experience of themselves feels unbearable, they will seek to cope with this – for instance by withdrawing, self-harming, drinking alcohol, etc.
- These strategies are understandable and work short term. Most of them are used by everyone at some time.
- Past trauma and the way that the body picks up threat signals and prepares for action combine to set up vicious circles that lock people into a trap.
- Where vicious circles are identified, the individual can choose to break them, and support and skills can be offered to help with this.

CCC offers a compassionate understanding of people's predicaments, along with ways forward that lend themselves to support– either from professionals or natural supporters such as family and friends. It is not another therapy brand, but represents an integration of third wave CBT approaches, on the theoretical foundation of the cognitive science based Interacting Cognitive Subsystems (ICS) model of cognitive architecture (Teasdale & Barnard, 1993). Thus it provides a pared down therapeutic approach applicable across diagnostic categories. It starts from the premise that all human beings, in all cultures, struggle at times with relationships (including the internal relationship with themselves), emotions and fitting in with the world around them. This is traceable to the way in which our brains operate. One part of our thinking apparatus gives us our sense of individual self-consciousness, and the ability to make precise judgements. Western cultures often over-value these aspects and underplay the functions of the other brain circuit. This gives us our emotions which enable us to relate to others and, internally, to ourselves. The crucial balance between these two brain circuits is held by state of arousal; the default, relational, circuit is more accessible at high and low arousal. High arousal can be experienced as emotion, or as physical disturbance, and it is this alteration in state of arousal which regulates relationship (see Clarke 2008, 2009, for a fuller exposition).

From this perspective, our very being is founded in relationship and we only make sense in the context of a web of relationships. Family and those close to us are clearly key to this, but it extends to the widest and deepest experience of relationship, the spiritual or religious. In emphasising the primacy of the emotional/relational aspect of the human being, CCC is in tune with non-Western cultures. Experience and felt sense are at the heart of the approach and 'symptoms' are viewed as understandable, but ultimately self-defeating, ways of coping with an intolerable internal state, which will have come about because of disruption in the web of roles and relationships that hold an individual together, and/or disruption in the crucial self/self relationship.

The training

Some of this complex trauma client group need, for reasons of risk and complexity, to be referred to Step 4 services. IAPT Step 2 (or whichever part of the service manages the initial assessment interview) needs the skills to identify and manage the interaction with this group. The training further equips Step 3 IAPT practitioners to recognise, engage and work effectively with those of this group who are suitable for Primary Care intervention.

Four one-day workshops are offered. Each group of practitioners attends three.

Day 1 is for Step 2: To develop the skills for recognising and managing complex trauma when this is present at assessment. To be able to distinguish cases of complex trauma suitable for Step 3.

Day 2 is for Step 3. To develop skills in recognition, motivation and engagement of people with a background of complex trauma, and to become familiar with the emotion focused formulation.

Day 3 is for Steps 2 and 3 working together. To understand the challenges of motivation and therapeutic alliance involved with working with this client group, and to acquire skills to manage these challenges, working from the individual formulation.

Day 4 is for Steps 2 and 3 working together. To use the formulation to identify the most appropriate interventions for particular patients, and to introduce a range of programmes incorporating suitable interventions.

This equips the staff to offer four individual, transdiagnostic, emotion-focused formulation sessions with an intensive 12 session group course, followed by one or two individual review sessions.

The group programme has been adopted in the four areas with enthusiasm and initial impressions and service user feedback are very promising. However, data collection has been slower due to commissioning pressures (the service has only just successfully weathered a retendering process). A full evaluation of the model as applied across Primary Care IAPT services in Hampshire is in preparation. Once its effectiveness has been properly established, we will be able to recommend this non-diagnostic intervention to the significant proportion of IAPT clients who have experienced complex trauma, and make it more widely available.

References

Clarke, I. (2008). Pioneering a cross-diagnostic approach founded in cognitive science. In I. Clarke & H. Wilson (Eds.), *Cognitive behavior therapy for acute inpatient mental health units: Working with clients, staff and the milieu* (pp.65–77). London: Routledge.

Clarke, I. (2009). Coping with crisis and overwhelming affect: Employing coping mechanisms in the acute inpatient context. In A.M. Columbus (Ed.), *Coping mechanisms: Strategies and outcomes* (pp.111–129). *Advances in Psychology Research, 63.* Huntington, NY State: Nova Science Publishers Inc. Available at: http://www.isabelclarke.org/docs/Coping_Mechanisms.doc

Clarke, I. (2015). The emotion focused formulation approach: Bridging individual and team formulation. *Clinical Psychology Forum, 275*, 28–32.

Durrant, C., Clarke, I., Tolland, A. & Wilson, H. (2007). Designing a CBT service for an acute in-patient setting: A pilot evaluation study. *Clinical Psychology and Psychotherapy, 14*, 117–125.

Teasdale, J.D. & Barnard, P.J. (1993). *Affect, cognition and change: Remodelling depressive thought.* Hove: Lawrence Erlbaum Associates.

Appendix 3

The Outcome-Oriented CAMHS model

The Outcome-Oriented CAMHS model has been developed and implemented in a community CAMHS team in Lincolnshire over a period of six years, led by Professor Sami Timimi (Timimi et al., 2013). It is based on understanding the evidence base on service outcomes in mental health where it is found that matching the model of treatment to a psychiatric diagnostic category has an insignificant impact. Therapy outcomes being achieved in studies 50 years ago are similar to those being achieved now. Moreover, there appears to be little difference in effectiveness between different therapy 'brands'. What does seem to be important within the therapy room is a meaningful therapeutic alliance; while external factors outside of treatment (the real life histories and contexts) such as socioeconomic status, motivation, the availability of a social network, and so on, are the most important contributors to outcomes.

A community Child and Adolescent Mental Health Services (CAMHS) team in Lincolnshire developed a new whole service model – the Outcome Orientated Child and Adolescent Mental Health Services (OO-CAMHS) model – which built on the principles of the 'Partners for Change Outcome Management Systems' (PCOMS) approach (Duncan, 2012). Based on the opposite principles to the diagnostic, 'model fidelity' ones, which are too often imposed in a rigid manner that alienates clinicians and lacks a credible evidence base (Bracken et al., 2012; Timimi, 2015a), the service builds on the belief that therapeutic interaction should honour the patient's voice, view mental suffering as part of the human dilemmas and challenges of being alive, and believe that positive change is possible. Staff in the service purposefully form partnerships to: (1) enhance the factors across theories that account for success – the so-called common factors of change; (2) use the patient's ideas and preferences to guide choice of approach; and (3) inform the work with reliable and valid measures of outcome and the patient's experience of the alliance.

Part of the model includes obtaining session-by-session or regular ratings of the young person's progress (as perceived by the young person themselves and/or their parents/carers) along with regular ratings of their experience of treatment. The model includes creating opportunities to discuss cases that are not improving in order to consider a change of approach or practitioner.

Because of the evidence that about 40 to 85 per cent of variance of outcome is accounted for by extra-therapeutic factors, such as social support, parental mental health, socio-economic status and motivation (Duncan et al., 2010; Wampold, 2001), exclusive individual work is only a small part of what is offered. Most clinicians also have to deal with pressures from the 'system' around the 'identified' patient. The OO-CAMHS model therefore also involves examining the system around the young person and team dynamics. It is not uncommon for a young person with problems, and their family, to have a variety of different organisations involved (such as school, specialist educational support, social services, parenting advisor, etc.) by the time that person is referred to CAMHS. Without proper consultation with the other agencies involved, subsequent intervention by CAMHS may be compromised. Not only may professionals be providing similar interventions, therefore unnecessarily duplicating work, but also the young person and their family may become confused and disempowered by conflicting advice and the increasing professionalisation of the problem. Thus, before embarking on treatment and during treatment, we think about the external factors/system around the patient, in order to avoid the risk of distancing people from their existing strengths and abilities, or of reinforcing feelings of vulnerability and lack of coping. We try to avoid more than one agency working on any one problem at any one time. We use professionals' meetings when one agency or more are already involved with the problem/issue the patient has been referred for.

It is not uncommon for agencies to imagine that a diagnosis will lead to a particular effective treatment, with the broader context being irrelevant to this process. Explanation that diagnosis in psychiatry simply describes sets of observed behaviours and reported experiences that often go together, but does not explain the cause or what treatment to use, is helpful (Timimi, 2013). This can open up opportunities for building on existing relationships with, for example, care staff and/or foster parents that may have been missed because of the mistaken belief that only specially trained professionals know how to deal with the young person's problems. Reducing to the minimum the number of professionals involved is often more empowering than increasing them. The patient and their family can be at the heart of discussions to inform the major stakeholders of their current needs and to direct future input from agencies.

The OO-CAMHS model is designed not just to support young patients and their families by putting them at the centre of their own care, but also to encourage team members to support each other. Professionals can then also build good and morale-boosting relationships in their working lives. Good therapy sees positive value, strengths, acceptance and abilities in their patients. Good teams see positive value, strengths, acceptance and abilities in their clinicians, supporting and respecting their autonomy and further training.

The service won an East Midlands Regional Innovation Fund award in November 2010 to help develop the model and implement it across the Lincolnshire CAMHS. It has since won a number of awards, including the Lincoln CAMHS team, the primary site of implementation, being runner-up in the British Medical Association Mental Health Team of the year in 2015. Unfortunately, the OO-CAMHS model was discontinued in April 2016, following commissioners mandating the implementation of a care pathway (therapy matched to specific diagnostic pathways) model in accordance with the national Children and Young People's Improving Access to Psychological Therapies (CYP-IAPT) approach (see Timimi 2015a, 2015b, for a critique of the CYP-IAPT model). By the time OO-CAMHS came to an end, it had been rolled out across Lincolnshire CAMHS teams. We had a database with outcomes recorded for over 4000 discharged cases where a reliable improvement and/or 'recovered' rate of 75 per cent were recorded. In a review of data in the Lincoln team comparing pre-OO-CAMHS implementation to two years post implementation, we found 'Did Not Attend' (DNA) rates had significantly reduced, outcomes had significantly improved, medication use had declined dramatically, and the proportion of cases which had been open to the team for more than two years reduced from 34 per cent of the case load to 18 per cent, indicating more successful discharges and fewer patients becoming 'chronic'.

Professor Sami Timimi, Consultant Child and Adolescent Psychiatrist, Lincolnshire Partnership Foundation NHS Trust.

References

Bracken, P., Thomas, P., Timimi, S. et al. (2012). Psychiatry beyond the current paradigm. *British Journal of Psychiatry, 201,* 430–434.

Duncan, B. (2012). The Partners for Change Outcome Management System (PCOMS): The Heart and Soul of Change Project. *Canadian Psychologist, 53,* 93–104.

Duncan, B., Miller, S., Wampold, B. & Hubble, M. (2010). *The heart and soul of change* (2nd edn.). Washington, DC: American Psychological Association.

Timimi, S. (2013). Non-diagnostic practice. *Context, 127,* 21–26.

Timimi, S. (2015a). Children and Young People's Improving Access to Psychological Therapies: Inspiring innovation or more of the same? *Psychiatric Bulletin, 39,* 57–60.

Timimi, S. (2015b). Update on the Improving Access to Psychological Therapies programme in England: Author's reply. *Psychiatric Bulletin, 39,* 252–253.

Timimi, S., Tetley, D., Burgoine, W. & Walker, G. (2013). Outcome Orientated Child and Adolescent Mental Health Services (OO-CAMHS): A whole service model. *Clinical Child Psychology and Psychiatry, 18,* 169–184.

Wampold, B.E. (2001). *The great psychotherapy debate: Models, methods, and findings.* Mahwah, NJ: Erlbaum.

Appendix 4

Team formulation

Team formulation, the process by which a group or team of professionals is facilitated to develop a shared formulation or hypothesis about the reasons for a service user's difficulties, is an increasingly common practice in all specialties (Johnstone, 2013). While the most common use is with service users who are perceived to be complex or 'stuck' (e.g. Summers, 2006), some services have integrated individual and team formulation into all parts of the care pathway, with associated staff training and documentation (Casares & Johnstone, 2015; Clarke, 2015; Dexter-Smith, 2015). Descriptions of team formulation practice in Adult, Older Adult, Intellectual Disability, Health, Forensic and Adolescent settings can be found in *Clinical Psychology Forum* November 2015 (download at https://shop.bps.org.uk/publications/publication-by-series/clinical-psychology-forum/clinical-psychology-forum-no-275-november-2015-extended-edition.html). For team formulation in neuropsychology work, see Wilson et al. (2009).

One of the longest-established projects is in the Older People's services in Tees Esk and Wear Valleys NHS Foundation Trust (Dexter-Smith, 2015). Individual and team formulation is used across 11 community teams and nine wards. All staff receive mandatory training in formulation, and there is a recognised process for developing skills in facilitating formulation meetings (Marshall & Craven-Staines, 2015). Another large-scale project covers the acute AMH services of Southern Health NHS Foundation Trust, where training in the non-diagnostic Emotion Focused Formulation Approach, developed by consultant clinical psychologist Isabel Clarke, has been delivered to over 200 staff of all professions, including managers (Clarke, 2015). The whole Trust now uses a formulation-based service based on the assumption that the behaviours underlying all mental health diagnoses are understandable attempts to manage intolerable internal states. This allows for selection from a 'menu' of first-stage interventions such as mindfulness and arousal management, which are taught in the 8 to 12 sessions Emotional Coping Skills Group at the heart of the programme. Non-stigmatising ways of understanding voices and other anomalous experiences are also introduced. If appropriate, service users can then undertake more in-depth trauma processing work.

While the structure and therapeutic model varies from service to service, team formulation is probably best understood as a form of staff consultation or supervision, in which counter-transference feelings of stuckness, frustration or confusion may be a central focus. As with other forms of supervision, it may not be appropriate or helpful to share the resulting discussion with the service user in its entirety, although a parallel process of one-to-one formulation should feed into the team version, and vice versa. Team formulation can also be very helpful if the service user is currently too distressed to talk about their personal history and contexts. In such situations, a tentative formulation may help to avoid default to a narrow medical approach, by containing the team until a fuller picture emerges. Service user perspectives and involvement can be maintained in a variety of ways such as having an SU rep in the formulation meetings; having SU reps on the formulation project group; doing joint training with SUs; and so on (see examples in *Clinical Psychology Forum* November 2015).

To date, the most strongly endorsed research finding is staff enthusiasm for this way of working (Cole et al., 2015; Hollingworth & Johnstone, 2014; Unadkat et al., 2015). In small-scale audits and evaluations, staff report a range of benefits, including increased understanding and empathy, more cohesive and supportive team working, reduced team disagreement, improved morale, more consistent intervention plans, and greater hopefulness about the possibility of recovery (summaries in Cole et al., 2015; DCP, 2011). Facilitating team formulation meetings is a complex and demanding task, and like any approach it can be done badly (Johnstone, 2013; Marshall & Craven-Staines, 2015). However, other things being equal, it would be expected that these benefits would translate into more compassionate and effective practice. This is supported by emerging evidence that team formulation can help to reduce staff burnout and incidents of 'challenging behaviour' in service users (Berry et al., 2009; Newman-Taylor & Sambrook, 2012); and can result in significant reductions in service user distress, along with significant increases in their confidence in self-management (Araci & Clarke, 2016). More research is needed into how service users experience the impacts of this approach, and whether it leads to specific outcomes such as reduced need for medication and admission, greater service user satisfaction, higher recovery rates, and so on.

Of particular relevance to the PTM Framework is the use of team formulation as an effective way of shifting cultures towards more psychosocial perspectives, by providing a containing structure within which staff can be supported to acknowledge the causal impact of relational and social adversities (Clarke, 2015; Johnstone et al., 2015). Practitioners have reported that team formulation can, without directly challenging the diagnostic model, lead to a gradual erosion of narrow medical thinking as trauma, abuse and adversity become subjects that can be discussed more openly, the impact of coercive interventions starts to be recognised, and the team becomes increasingly sophisticated at translating 'symptoms' and 'illnesses' into understandable responses to life circumstances (Dexter-Smith, 2015; Johnstone, 2013; Johnstone et al., 2015).

References

Araci, D. & Clarke, I. (2016). Investigating the efficacy of a whole team, psychologically informed, acute mental health service approach. *Journal of Mental Health.* doi:10.3109/09638237.2016.1139065

Berry, K., Barrowclough, C. & Wearden, A. (2009). A pilot study investigating the use of psychological formulations to modify psychiatric staff perceptions of service users with psychosis. *Behavioural and Cognitive Psychotherapy, 37,* 39–48.

Clarke, I. (2015). The Emotion Focused Formulation Approach: Bridging individual and team formulation. *Clinical Psychology Forum, 275,* 28–32.

Cole, S., Wood, K. & Spendelow, J. (2015). Team formulation: A critical evaluation of current literature and future research directions. *Clinical Psychology Forum, 275,* 13–19.

Dexter-Smith, S. (2015). Implementing psychological formulations service-wide. *Clinical Psychology Forum, 275,* 43–54.

Division of Clinical Psychology (2011). *Good Practice Guidelines on the use of psychological formulation.* Leicester: British Psychological Society.

Hollingworth, P. & Johnstone, L. (2014). Team formulation: What are the staff views? *Clinical Psychology Forum, 257,* 28–34.

Johnstone, L. (2013). Using formulation in teams. In L. Johnstone & R. Dallos (Eds.), *Formulation in psychology and psychotherapy: Making sense of people's problems* (2nd edn., pp.216–242). London: Routledge.

Johnstone, L., Durrant, C., James, L. et al. (2015). Team formulation developments in AMH services in South Wales. *Clinical Psychology Forum, 275,* 38–42.

Marshall, J. & Craven-Staines, S. (2015). Developing the use of a formulation session reflection tool in mental health services for older people. *Clinical Psychology Forum, 275,* 69–74.

Newman-Taylor, K. & Sambrook, S. (2012). CBT for culture change: Formulating teams to improve patient care. *Behavioural and Cognitive Psychotherapy, 40,* 496–503.

Summers, A. (2006). Psychological formulations in psychiatric care: Staff views on their impact. *Psychiatric Bulletin, 30,* 34–352.

Unadkat, S.N., Irving Quinn, G., Jones, F. et al. (2015). Staff experiences of formulating within a team setting. *Clinical Psychology Forum, 275,* 85–88.

Wilson, B.A., Gracey, F., Evans, J.J. & Bateman, A. (2009). *Neuropsychological rehabilitation: Theory, models, therapy and outcome.* Cambridge: Cambridge University Press.

Appendix 5

Groupwork for women survivors of abuse

Group Trauma Focused Therapy for women survivors of childhood sexual abuse has been offered continuously over the last three decades in Exeter, Devon. The SAGE (Sexual Abuse Groups Exeter) trauma processing groupwork draws from feminist theory and therapy (Brown 2004; Herman, 2001; Mendelsohn et al., 2011; Watson et al., 1996) and forms one of the psychological therapies provided by the adult mental health services within Devon Partnership NHS Trust. High levels of abuse in childhood are disclosed by women with severe and complex mental health distress referred to adult mental health services. Women are offered individual trauma therapy prior to a SAGE group in order to be able to disclose their experience of abuse safely and begin to establish effective strategies for managing distress. The groups offer the possibility of lessening shame and isolation and of being heard and understood. This Trauma Focused Group Therapy has recently been extended to Cwm Taf Health Board, South Wales, under the name SAFE (Sexual Abuse: Freedom and Empowerment), where it is now offered to women in both primary and secondary adult mental health services in locations across all four valleys in the catchment area.

The SAGE and SAFE groups are attended by a maximum of six women, and are facilitated by two trained women workers. The two-and a half hour sessions take place over 12 weeks, with follow-ups at one and six months. Each woman also has a designated individual therapy support worker (ITSW) who meets her weekly to help process the material arising from the group. Group facilitators and ITSWs receive ongoing supervision, and the supportive structure for both workers and group attenders enables the intense trauma processing work of the groups to be provided safely and effectively.

Group therapy is acknowledged as being particularly effective in helping women to address the effects of childhood sexual abuse such as trauma symptoms, isolation, stigma, shame, self-blame and re-victimisation (Higgins Kessler et al., 2003; Walker & Rosen, 2004). In Judith Herman's words, trauma focused group work 're-creates a sense of belonging; where trauma degrades the victim, the group praises them, and wherein trauma dehumanises the victim, the group restores humanity' (Herman, 2001, p.214). The mutual empathy and connection that emerge within the groups offer a very powerful forum within which women can break the secrecy, isolation, shame and silencing of abuse. The groups legitimise the profound distress and damage of childhood abuse and open up the possibility of expressing, in comparative safety, their long standing grief, loss, sadness and anger. The mental health distress that women have experienced over many years becomes understandable as a consequence of abuse.

Local evaluations of SAGE and SAFE have consistently identified significant reductions in measures of depression, trauma symptoms, shame, self-harm, suicidal thoughts, prescribed medication use and alcohol/substance abuse. Corresponding increases in self-worth scores are reported post group and maintained at six month follow-up. Qualitative feedback elicits comments such as: 'I feel I was heard and I was comforted and the feeling of being accepted despite all the abuse is so powerful.'

SAGE and SAFE are time intensive, but local evaluations have shown them to be cost effective, with savings on inpatient bed use and decrease in secondary mental health service. In addition, MDT staff report that their involvement is a highly rewarding experience which has increased their general trauma work skills. The groups have helped to embed trauma-informed thinking within the MDTs and have led to a number of other developments, such as a peer support group for survivors of abuse, and the opportunity for graduates of the groups to be involved in staff training. In Exeter, some of the former group attenders have taken up roles within the SAGE service.

Stabilisation Pack

As part of the development of trauma informed services, clinical psychologists in Cwm Taf Adult Mental Health Services have developed a 'Stabilisation Pack' of psycho-educational resource for people who have experienced complex trauma. The pack is divided into 14 handouts that explain how trauma and adversity of all kinds can contribute to a range of mental health difficulties, such as hearing voices, unusual beliefs, dissociation, mood swings and self harm, which can be seen as understandable consequences and/or survival strategies. The handouts thus offer an alternative understanding to the biomedical model, along with a range of coping skills such as grounding, soothing skills, distraction, and crisis planning. The pack has been developed into an eight week stabilisation course, and outcome data suggest an improvement in Core-34 scores and a reduction in trauma symptoms. Evaluation also shows that staff feel the pack has increased their knowledge and confidence in stage 1 trauma work, and it is used widely within the community AMH teams.

The stabilisation pack is available at: http://cwmtaf.wales/services/mental-health/stabilisation-pack/

References

Herman, J. (2001). *Trauma and recovery*. New York: Basic Books.

Brown, L.S. (2004). Feminist paradigms of trauma treatment. *Psychotherapy: Theory, Research Practice & Training, 41*, 464–471.

Higgins Kessler, M.R., White, B.M. & Nelson, B.S. (2003). Group treatments for women sexually abused as children: A review of the literature and recommendations for future research. *Child Abuse and Neglect, 27*, 1045–1061.

Mendelsohn, M., Herman, J.L., Schatzow, E. et al. (2011). *The trauma recovery group: A guide for practitioners*. New York: Guilford Press.

Walker, M. & Rosen, W. B. (2004). *How connections heal: Stories from relational cultural therapy*. New York: Guilford Press.

Watson, G., Scott, C. & Ragalsky, S. (1996) . Refusing to be marginalised: Groupwork in mental health services for women survivors of childhood sexual abuse. *Journal of Community and Applied Social Psychology, 6*, 341–354.

Appendix 6

Pathways in Forensic Work

The 'Offender Personality Disorder' (OPD) Pathway is a national strategy for men and women who are classed as high risk by criminal justice colleagues and who present with indications that they could be diagnosed as having a 'personality disorder.' The pathway is co-commissioned by NHS England and the National Offender Management Service (NOMS) meaning that health and probation are working in partnership to enhance the criminal justice management of this client group. The OPD Pathway consists of a number of different services across the country and aims to increase the psychological wellbeing of service users, to increase capacity for working with this client group through workforce development and to reduce the frequency and severity of sexual and violent offending. The work is founded on the principle that the management of the client group is best kept within criminal justice services. Despite the official terminology, which is not our choice or preference, there is also an emphasis on psychologically-informed case management support and on formulation. The pathway therefore offers an opportunity to de-emphasise diagnosis and recognise the complex, often trauma-related causal factors that are linked to offending.

The work of the Yorkshire Humberside Personality Disorder Partnership is described below.

While the pathway is described in diagnostic terms, eligible men and women do not have to have a formal diagnosis, and it is intended that the case management is led by individualised formulations. We have therefore used the pathway as an opportunity for working from a psychosocially and systemically-informed perspective, within an area that has traditionally been dominated by an individualised, decontextualised medical model.

Our conceptualisation of the problems associated with a personality disorder diagnosis is based on an understanding that:

- individuals who have been given a diagnosis of 'personality disorder' are not a homogenous group;
- the reactions and behaviours associated with this label can be understood primarily as a consequence of adverse developmental experiences (Livesley, 2003);
- these consequences often include significant and long-lasting difficulties with self identity and relationships;
- these difficulties frequently arise out of lack of opportunity to develop mentalising or reflective capacity;
- organisations confront powerful and primitive emotional states when engaged in helping relationships (Obholzer & Roberts, 1994) meaning that the care, management or treatment of individuals with a diagnosis of 'personality disorder' may be, in itself, harmful or iatrogenic;
- The widest possible social perspective should be used (Pilgrim, 2001) so as to respond therapeutically to the myriad of different ways in which the people so diagnosed may struggle with their lives, social circumstances, employment, health and wellbeing.

The team consists of psychologists/psychotherapists, occupational therapists and specialist Offender Managers. We are aiming, broadly speaking, to create a thinking system (a system which can think about minds) through consultation and training and to involve relevant people in this collaborative process. We also offer individual and group work, psychoeducation, and occupational therapy with the overarching aim of facilitating engagement, fostering attachments and creating the conditions for increasing reflectiveness. Psychoeducation is a core part of our intensive intervention risk management services and, wherever possible and appropriate, we try and help people to think about the roots of their difficulties in early trauma. Therapeutic options include schema and CFT work, delivered in groups or individually, and a year-long Mentalisation Based Therapy (MBT) programme. In addition, we promote Psychologically Informed Planned Environments (PIPEs) within probation hostels.

The focus for our work is often not 'treatment' in the traditional sense since our clients may not be ready to engage in this way. Rather, they may need us to understand that they have lived – often every day of their lives – with hatred, anger, hostility and violence, in the context of chaotic, abusive and exploitative social contexts. Our task is to help them to move towards a more complex and reflective understanding of their own motivations, emotions and behaviour as well as those of other people. However, a large part of our work is with those who are in their lives – the individuals and organisations they currently have relationships with. While we ask clients to hold a complex understanding of those interactions, we also require organisations and professionals to do the same. We believe that many problems associated with the diagnosis of 'personality disorder' involve an organisation's inability to identify and contain emotional reactions not just of the client but of workers. Our work is, therefore, about helping systems and organisations to think about their own minds as well as the service user's.

The work is relatively new, but so far there are signs that it can be helpful in developing competencies for working with this client group. There is some evidence that recalls back to prison are better managed and reduced, and that relationships with service users have been enhanced.

Jo Ramsden, Consultant Clinical Psychologist

References

Baker, V., Ramsden, J. & Wood, J. (2016). Psychology working in partnership with probation: Giving away the family silver? *Clinical Psychology Forum, 268,* 42–45.

Livesley, W.J. (2003). *Practical management of personality disorder.* New York & London: Guilford Press.

Obholzer, A. & Roberts, V.Z. (Eds.) (1994). *The unconscious at work: Individual and organizational stress in the human services.* London: Routledge.

Pilgrim, D. (2001). Disordered personalities, disordered concepts. *Journal of Mental Health, 10,* 253–265.

Appendix 7

Trauma-informed pathways in Adult Mental Health

Tees Esk and Wear Valleys NHS Foundation Trust (TEWV) is a large mental health provider in the North of England which serves a population of two million people and employs over 6700 staff. The Trust has recently invested in a formal Trauma Informed Care Project to set up the resources and structures necessary for it to address the trauma-related needs of the people who use its services. This emerged from the successful development and piloting of trauma informed care within the adult division, with consultant clinical psychologist Angela Kennedy as Pathway Lead.

TEWV, like most Adult Mental Health services in England, uses 'pathways' to describe the structures, management systems and decision-making necessary to support the needs of a specific client group. Most of these pathways are diagnostically based. However, the addition of a Clinical Link Pathway for Trauma now allows for trauma-informed intervention for anyone who needs it regardless of their diagnosis. The Link is an adjunct to other care and for some people will become the main focus of their support. This means that all service users can be assessed for trauma at first contact, and offered trauma-informed interventions such as information, stabilisation and therapy if and when indicated. Formulation and team formulation are built into the core processes, along with opportunities for specialist consultation and supervision.

The pilot project on an acute adult mental health ward included all staff from senior medics to health care assistants. They found that three quarters of the people admitted could directly link trauma with their current difficulties. With support and training, ward staff felt empowered to have meaningful discussions about trauma and used this to inform formulation-based care plans. They were able to implement some core skills in grounding and emotion regulation, which resulted in a reduction in the use of medication. Staff could also call on external complex case consultation, which was evaluated as being extremely helpful.

Following on from this successful pilot, the trauma-informed approach began to be disseminated throughout the service, with local trauma champions facilitating supervision, management and implementation of the guidance. Training is undertaken as a team and it has been well received with most staff reporting it relevant to their work and increasing their confidence afterwards. Resources include information leaflets for clients, their families and carers; resource links and summaries for staff; a treatment algorithm; service skills matrix; good practice guidance for managing trauma disclosures; information on screening for dissociation and how to manage it; a section on staff wellbeing; and a framework for understanding risk issues. Trauma-specific supervision groups and training are supporting therapists to respond to issues of complex trauma. TEWV has engaged experts by experience, including activist and trainer Jacqui Dillon, to deliver or co-produce the training.

Introduction of the trauma-informed approach has not been quick or easy, and it has taken a great deal of planning, patience and determination to keep it on the agenda in spite of organisational changes, mergers and competing priorities. Although the ultimate aim is to implement the approach across all inpatient and community services, there has inevitably been more progress in some areas than others. Recently the Trust has committed to developing this approach in all specialities, including offender health, children's services, services for older people, etc.

A few key factors have facilitated the ambitious scope and success so far. First, it was important to sell the concept to senior leaders in the organisation, including the medical director, using language that connected with its change processes and key objectives. Unidentified trauma was demonstrated, using local statistics and service user stories (e.g. three-quarters of the Trust's AMH inpatients feel trauma is a significant factor in their difficulties) to be impeding recovery, and the project is now a Trust strategic priority. It was also important that staff felt empowered rather than burdened by the change. The new pathway is flexible, allowing for varying therapeutic approaches and patient choice. The process of embedding trauma-informed practice will be gradual over time as awareness deepens and skills assimilate. In evaluations, staff have reported that relatively simple interventions and small changes of attitude have had a major positive impact. Most importantly, the personal voices and experiences of service users have been vital in showing the way.

Angela Kennedy, Consultant Clinical Psychologist

Appendix 8

Formulation-based work as an alternative to diagnosis in the Middle East

The United Nations Relief and Works Agency for Palestine Refugees (UNRWA)) was established by the UN General Assembly in 1949 and mandated to provide assistance and protection to some five million registered Palestine refugees living in 58 official UN refugee camps in Jordan, Lebanon, Syria, West Bank and the Gaza Strip. UNRWA services encompass education, health care, welfare/relief and social services, camp infrastructure and improvement, and microfinance. Dating back 65 years, this is one of the most protracted refugee crises in the world. The refugee camps are extremely overcrowded with poor sanitation, limited electricity, deteriorating infrastructure and increasing levels of poverty and food insecurity. Palestinian refugee communities have few social or civic rights and no access to public social facilities. Palestinian refugees are continuously exposed to violence of different types, within the family, within the communities and within a context of hostility from surrounding populations with little or no prospect of a resolution to their political situation and legal status.

In Gaza, the blockade by Israel and security forces is now in its ninth year. There are regular armed conflicts with heavy causalities and destruction of infrastructure, including schools, hospitals, water and electricity facilities, and so on. Poverty is high, and unemployment is estimated to be the highest globally. Fifty per cent of Gaza's population are under 18 years old and most are unlikely ever to be employed. Children, adults and families know only life under occupation, repeated wars, economic blockade, fear, violence and enduring hardship, with the vast majority never having left or been allowed to leave Gaza.

UNRWA has a Community Mental Health Programme in Gaza which provides a wide range of services targeting children, young people, parents, older adults and persons with disabilities, as well as local communities, local people's committees and local organisations. The programme has been in operation since 2002. There are over 250 school counsellors working with children, families and local communities and another 23 health counsellors based in the health clinics across the Gaza Strip.

In Lebanon, UNRWA's services also include psychosocial support and mental health, spanning five regional areas within Lebanon, each with a very varied political, social and economic landscape. The recent Syrian war has led to the displacement of Palestinian refugees in UN refugee camps in Syria, now moved to refugee camps in Lebanon. The intense crowding has contributed to inter-communal and family violence, abuse, increased poverty and further instability.

All UNWRA frontline staff in Gaza and Lebanon working in these camps are also Palestinian refugees – often living the same conditions and hardships as experienced by other Palestinian refugees.

In this context, emotional and psychological distress is an understandable response to the many adversities and threats that people face on a daily basis. In 2012 Professor

Nimisha Patel, Director, International Centre for Health and Human Rights, was invited to help develop psychosocial services within UNRWA, first in Gaza and then in Lebanon. Her work, specifically in Gaza and Lebanon UNWRA refugee camps, aims to provide a more meaningful and context-appropriate alternative to the previously diagnosis-driven approach influenced by Western researchers and consultants and more recently, by the World Health Organisation's diagnosis-based Mental Health Gap Action Programme (mhGAP), which aims to 'scale up' services for mental health problems in low and middle-income countries (http://www.who.int/mental_health/mhgap/en/).

Gaza: Since 2012, Professor Patel has trained 20 UNRWA school counsellors in Gaza in a range of skills including psychosocial assessments and the development and use of formulations to guide their work. Each of these 20 school counsellors was then trained to be a supervisor, and they in turn trained other counsellors working in health centres and in all UN schools in Gaza. In total, nearly 300 counsellors working in schools and health centres are now trained in and use formulations in their daily work with children, adults and families. Where previously counsellors routinely used diagnoses, they now use an approach which is explicitly formulation-led. Professor Patel has revised all supporting documentation, including assessment forms for children and adults (including a specific section and prompts for developing formulations), risk assessment protocols, databases and case records sheets, so that rather than recording diagnoses, they provide opportunities to consider and revise the working formulation at every stage of the intervention.

Lebanon: As in Gaza, in Lebanon Professor Patel has trained 20 UNRWA staff to use formulation as an alternative to diagnosis in all their work. This has included senior staff nurses (not mental health nurses) in health clinics (equivalent to general practice/family health centres); school counsellors; and senior social workers. In turn, they have trained, under her supervision and constant guidance, all social workers in UNRWA across Gaza (over 60), all school counsellors (now amounting to 200), and all staff nurses and senior staff nurses (over 40) on how to develop psychosocial formulations. Although they all have the standard five days' mhGAP training in diagnosis, their documentation (assessment forms, client records, risk assessments, etc.) and daily practice is based exclusively on psychosocial formulations, with diagnoses only being used by psychiatrists (where available) or family doctors.

Formulation work in context

The range of problems is very wide, but in children typically includes the impact of violence and abuse, and the consequences of living in families coping with poverty, unemployment, poor housing, multiple traumas, losses and bereavements. Adults are struggling with very intense ongoing states of fear and grief, interpersonal and community violence (often gender-based), and general conflict-related threats and insecurity.

Staff are trained to use 'The Assessment and Formulation Wheel' (below) for each referral. They are encouraged to make repeat circles of the wheel with the client, listing hypotheses and exploration and intervention points.

Child, Adult, Family – in context: Assessment and formulation wheel

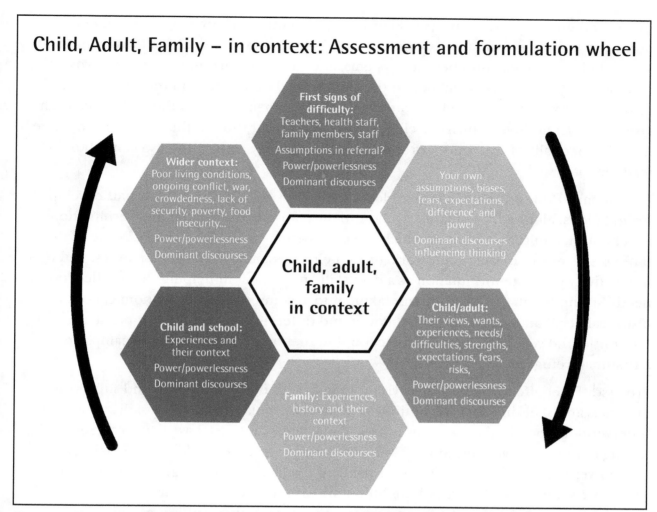

Figure 2: Child, Adult, Family – in context: Assessment and formulation wheel. © Nimisha Patel, 2012

Formulating and meaning-making in context

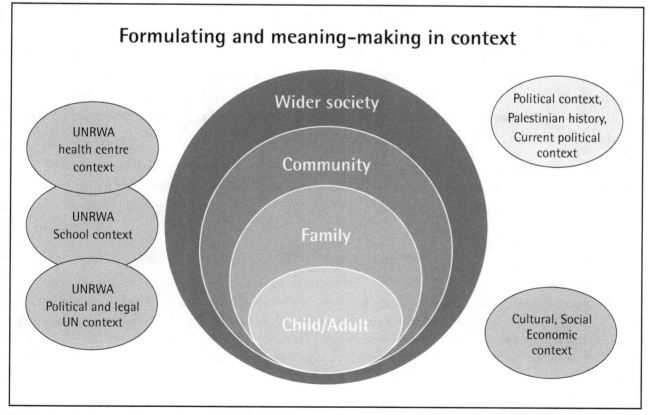

Figure 3: Formulating fand meaning-making in context. © Nimisha Patel, 2012

The staff then use the diagram (see Figure 3), populating the circles with bullet points, notes and meanings from the Assessment and Formulation wheel. This allows them to add arrows linking relationships between systems, and noting recurrent themes, patterns and experiences (which may be echoed in the professional's own life, and thus often painful to acknowledge). It is essential to note the wider discourses and how they influence each system/level, and how in turn the client, family, staff resist those influences. The concrete material inequalities and injustices and the meanings they convey are also central to the formulation.

In summary, Professor Patel has provided a framework to help the trained staff develop formulations, along with guidance on how to develop case discussions and formulations for children, adults and families, which are used systematically for all cases. None of the staff uses diagnosis in their daily work, or in their assessment forms or case notes, and they now actively promote formulation as a core skill and a 'tool' in helping them reflect on the needs, strengths, etc., of Palestinians, taking into account the social, economic, political, historical, legal and cultural context. Power and difference, and gender in particular, are considered very explicitly, and are central to their experiences living in camps and as Palestinian refugees.

Professor Patel offers ongoing supervision to help staff develop training and supervision materials and skills in order to continue to embed formulation as a core skill and a core 'intervention/tool' in their work as nurses, counsellors and social workers. Staff report feeling empowered with additional skills in formulating and emboldened to make sense of their very complex cases, without resorting to medicalised language and diagnoses. They have stated that when they have little time with their clients, offering a formulation provides 'comfort, relief and a feeling that we understand their suffering – and this builds trust and they make most use of the time we can offer them, they are grateful we spend time to properly understand instead of giving them basic food or medication and sending them away.' Nurses have reported: 'We can be real nurses, not just injecting and giving basic help, but we give them time, listen, and we try to make sense of their situation with them. They feel we want to understand.' Similarly, social workers have said that formulations help them to 'finally do social work as we want to do, the way we have to do – understanding psychological distress in the complex social and political context we all live in.' More formal evaluations are currently at the planning stage.

These ongoing projects have shown that it is possible to implement non-diagnostic, formulation-based practice across health, education and welfare services in communities experiencing widespread distress in the face of extreme and continuing adversities.

Related reading

Patel, N. (in press). The mantra of 'Do no harm' in international healthcare responses to refugee people. In B. Drozdek & T. Wenzel (Eds.), *The health of refugees: An interdisciplinary perspective.* London: Springer.

Patel, N. (2011). The psychologisation of torture. In M. Rapley, J. Moncrieff & J. Dillon (Eds.), *De-medicalising misery: Psychiatry, psychology and the human condition* (pp.239–255). London: Palgrave Macmillan.

Patel, N. & Mahtani, A. (2007). The politics of working with refugee survivors of torture. *The Psychologist, 20,* 164–166.

Appendix 9

Narrative approaches

The narrative metaphor has influenced therapists from different traditions, but what they have in common is the idea that it is beneficial to develop 'rich' stories about one's life which offer opportunities for change (Angus & McLeod, 2004; Polkinghorne, 2004; White, 2004). When people seek professional help, their lives have often become single storied, limiting, limited and superficial rather than richly textured and multiply storied (White & Epston, 1990). Especially if they have had contact with mental health systems, these stories may have become problem-saturated and pathologising, and individualising labels are likely to have been internalised. A central process is therefore to engage the client in evaluating emerging narratives by inviting them to stand back from dominant stories and to make choices about whether they enhance and enrich their lives or else limit and diminish them. The aim is to help people see that they have options of which they were previously unaware. Thus, someone might be encouraged to question the dominant narrative of being 'mentally ill' or 'schizophrenic' and reclaim other aspects of their identity. Moreover, in order to develop criteria by which to judge these stories, clients become more aware of their values and how they wish to live their lives. The approach has been used in various settings, including intellectual disability (Lyngaarrd & Scior, 2002) and neuropsychology (Weatherhead & Todd, 2014).

Michael White and David Epston, social workers and founders of narrative therapy, use various ways of encouraging different kinds of conversations which might in turn open up alternative meanings of distress. For example, while they were interested in the history of the problem and the dominant narrative, they also aimed to plot a history of new, previously hidden alternative stories. However, because they saw stories building on internal state or trait concepts as inherently limiting, they drew on Jerome Bruner's notion of intentional narratives, encouraging people to develop stories which featured purposes, values, beliefs, hopes, dreams, visions and commitments to ways of living rather than on internal states like 'strengths' (a concept which is dependent on the notion of weakness in order to have any meaning). These conversations might identify the traces of more marginalised or subordinated stories, which broke with the dominant narrative and which would be experienced by clients as enhancing the way they saw themselves and increasing the options available to them in their lives.

One way of elaborating these stories is to engage in a process of scaffolding – a notion developed by theorists following Vygotsky's (1978) concept of the zone of proximal development. Here, particular questions are asked in order to support (or 'scaffold') the development of emerging stories. Another strategy is to use 'externalising conversations' in which clients are encouraged to distance themselves from messages of personal deficit and to unite with the therapist, and perhaps with others in their family or social network, in order to challenge unhelpful dominant narratives.

The key aim in narrative therapy is thus to promote the development of rich, multiply storied and intentional narratives – sometimes called 'thick description'. These can be contrasted with the more superficial 'thin' descriptions afforded by, for example, psychiatric diagnostic labels, and with causal explanations framed in terms of 'factors' like internalised psychological processes. Influenced by Michel Foucault's work on the links between power and knowledge, White and Epston were also concerned with the ways in which particular views of the world are embodied in institutions, and how people and their stories are regulated by the normalising gaze of society. Narrative therapy thus provides a basis for developing stories which engage actively with inequalities and injustice. For example, the 'Just Therapy' movement, developed in New Zealand within the narrative tradition, has an explicit focus on the historical and ongoing injustices suffered by the Maori and Samoan peoples (Waldegrave, 1990, 2009). It is committed to cultural, gender and socio-economic equality, and has been influential in many other therapeutic fields (http://www.familycentre.org.nz/Areas_of_Work/Family_Therapy).

References

Angus, L.E. & McLeod, J. (Eds.) (2004). *The handbook of narrative and psychotherapy: Practice, theory and research.* London: Sage.

Lyngaarrd, H. & Scior, K. (2002). Narrative therapy and people with learning difficulties. *Clinical Psychology, 17,* 33–36.

Polkinghorne, D.E. (2004). Narrative therapy and postmodernism. In L.E. Angus & J. McLeod (Eds.) *The handbook of narrative and psychotherapy: Practice, theory and research* (pp.53–67). London: Sage.

Vygotsky, L.S. (1978). *Mind in society: The development of higher psychological processes.* London: Harvard University Press.

Waldegrave, C. (1990). Just therapy. *Dulwich Centre Newsletter, 1,* 5–46.

Waldegrave, C. (2009). Cultural, gender and socio-economic contexts in therapeutic and social policy work. *Family Process, 48,* 85–101.

Weatherhead, S. & Todd, D. (2014). *Narrative approaches to brain injury.* London: Karnac.

White, M. & Epston, D. (1990). *Narrative means to therapeutic ends.* London: Norton.

White, M. (2004). Folk psychology and narrative practice. In L.E. Angus, & J. McLeod (Eds.), *The handbook of narrative and psychotherapy: Practice, theory and research* (pp.15–51). London: Sage.

Appendix 10

Open Dialogue

Open Dialogue is a family and social network-centred intervention which has been developed by psychologist Jaakko Seikkula and colleagues over the last 30 years, initially in response to high prevalence of individuals with the diagnosis of 'schizophrenia' in Western Lapland. It is now used as the basis of mental health care across the whole area, and projects have been set up in a number of other countries including the rest of Scandinavia, Germany and several states in the US. Open Dialogue is widely claimed to achieve the best documented outcomes for 'psychosis' in the Western world.

Open Dialogue has a focus on crisis-resolution and a quick response following referral. The intervention consists of a series of open meetings between the service user or individual referred, their family and others in their social network or support system, and two to three staff members trained in psychotherapy, who might include psychiatrists, psychologists, and nurses. Its seven guiding principles are: immediate help within 24 hours of referral or contact with the team; a social networks perspective including, for example, colleagues or friends; flexibility and mobility which includes needs-based adaption of the therapeutic response and/or location of meetings; responsibility of the staff team who works with the family across the course of the intervention; psychological continuity, whereby meetings continue to be held for as long as is necessary and across outpatient and inpatient care if necessary; tolerance of uncertainty, whereby a safe space is created for the team, the individual and their network, and premature decisions or conclusions are avoided; and finally, the promotion of dialogism as a primary concern, empowering families with a sense of agency (Seikkula & Arnkil, 2014).

Open Dialogue is based on the recognition that no-one exists in isolation, and that problems and solutions are socially constructed through shared language and understandings. Rather than identifying deficits within the individual, problems are seen as emerging within the social network (Seikkula et al., 2003). It is accepted that there is no ultimate 'truth' – rather, there are a number of truths, each held by a different voice. Philosophically, Open Dialogue draws from social constructionism, systemic family therapy, and dialogical theory, and in particular the ideas of literary theorist Mikhail Bakhtin (see also Appendix 9 'Narrative Approaches'). He argued that language is inherently dialogical, in that an idea always arises in dialogue with and response to other ideas, which sets a context for subsequent ideas. This means that in practice, rather than trying to develop one single narrative about what has happened, the team seeks to understand different possible interpretations and meanings through conversation. These meanings can only emerge if all contributions are acknowledged and all voices unconditionally accepted, with the team being willing to tolerate uncertainty, refrain from interrupting or interpreting, and hold the strong emotions in the room. There is no rush to make decisions, even in severe distress, since it is accepted that understanding is a gradual, organic process. Over time, the social network develops its own resources. There is an opportunity to retell people's stories, and in doing so, explore new identities and rebuild relationships. In this way, crises can become an opportunity for positive change.

Three outcome studies for the approach have been published, although these were naturalistic studies rather than randomised control trials. The initial study suggested that across a two-year follow-up period, in comparison with a treatment as usual (TAU) group who had diagnoses of 'schizophrenia', the Open Dialogue groups had shorter hospitalisations and were prescribed less neuroleptic medication (Seikkula et al., 2003). During early stages of the approach, groups from the initial two phases of development (1992–3 and 1994–7) were compared over a five-year follow-up period. Findings showed that the second group had fewer days in hospital and fewer family meetings as the programme was developed. The outcomes were broadly similar across the two Open Dialogue groups, and showed better outcomes in comparison with a Swedish five-year follow-up TAU study (Svedberg et al., 2001). Twenty-nine per cent of the second Open Dialogue group used neuroleptic medication in the course of treatment, compared with 93 per cent in the TAU study, and 86 per cent had returned to studies or full-time work with 14 per cent on disability allowance, compared with 62 per cent of the TAU study patients who were on disability allowance at the end of follow-up (Seikkula et al., 2006). A further study (Seikkula et al., 2011) compared the earlier two phases of Open Dialogue intervention with one from a later period, in order to assess the consistency of findings across a 10-year period. All the groups that had received the Open Dialogue intervention had similar percentages of people back in full-time employment or study at follow-up (84 per cent).

A randomised control trial is currently underway at four sites in the UK, led by a team at University College London (http://www.nelft.nhs.uk/aboutus-initiatives-opendialogue). A three-year training programme has also been set up in London http://opendialogueapproach.co.uk/

Further reading

http://open-dialogue.net/

http://developingopendialogue.com/

https://www.youtube.com/watch?v=AxGPcSPR04c

References

Hopfenbeck, M. (2015). Peer-supported open dialogue. *Context, 138*, 29–31.

Seikkula, J., Alakare, B., Aaltonen, J. et al. (2003). Open dialogue approach: Treatment principles and preliminary results of a two-year follow-up on first episode schizophrenia. *Ethical and Human Sciences and Services, 5*, 163–182.

Seikkula, J., Aaltonen, J., Alakare, B. et al. (2006). Five-year experience of first-episode nonaffective psychosis in open-dialogue approach: Treatment principles, follow-up outcomes, and two case studies. *Psychotherapy Research, 16*, 214–228.

Seikkula, J., Alakare, B. & Aaltonen, J. (2011). The Comprehensive Open-Dialogue Approach in Western Lapland: II. Long-term stability of acute psychosis outcomes in advanced community care. *Psychosis, 3*, 192–204.

Seikkula, J. & Arnkil, T.E. (2014). *Open dialogues and anticipations: Respecting otherness in the present moment.* Helsinki: THL Publications.

Svedberg, B., Mesterton, A. & Cullberg, J. (2001). First-episode non-affective psychosis in a total urban population: A five-year follow-up. *Social Psychiatry and Psychiatric Epidemiology, 36*, 332–337.

Appendix 11

The Hearing Voices Network

The Hearing Voices Network (HVN) is an influential, grassroots organisation, which works to promote acceptance and understanding of hearing voices, seeing visions and other unusual sensory experiences. HVN is a collaboration between experts by experience (voice-hearers and family members) who work in partnership with experts by profession (academics, clinicians and activists) to question, critique, and reframe traditional biomedical understandings of voice-hearing. It originated in the work of Marius Romme, a Dutch psychiatrist, who was challenged by his client Patsy Hage to take her voices seriously as a real experience for her. He and science journalist Sandra Escher have published several influential books on working and living with voices (Romme & Escher, 1998, 2000). As the limits of a solely medical approach to hearing voices and other unusual perceptions has become more widely known, and people are better informed about alternatives, there has been a growing acceptance by mainstream mental health providers of this approach. HVN in England now has more than 180 groups operating in many conventional mental health settings, including child and adolescent mental health services, prisons, inpatient units, secure units as well as in community settings. There are 33 other national HVNs, spread across Europe, North America, Australia, New Zealand, Latin America and Africa.

The position advocated by HVN, that hearing voices and other unusual sensory perceptions are common human experiences for which there are many explanations, is in contrast to the dominant medical discourse. Finding a safe, confidential space to share your experiences with other people who are accepting of you and your voices, trying to understand the meaning of these experiences in order to make better peace with them, can be a transformative and healing experience.

Although the experience of hearing voices is solitary, complex and varies from person to person, there are themes which seem to be common for many voice hearers, across cultures. 'Living with Voices: 50 Stories of Recovery', an anthology of testimonies from voice hearers from all over the world, demonstrated that even though each person's account was entirely unique, there were a number of key themes which emerged from all of the stories: that the voices were often a survival strategy, that the voices were deemed significant, decipherable and intimately connected to the hearer's life story, that voices sometimes used metaphorical language and that healing was not contingent on banishing the voices but was about understanding their meaning, improving communication with the voices and consequently, having a more positive relationship with them (Romme et al., 2009).

The HVN does not offer a therapeutic model. It uses diverse strategies to promote change, including self-help groups, recovery and coping models, psychosocial formulation, social/ political activism, narrative approaches, and sharing hopeful, positive information.
It emphasises the right of individuals to hold their own beliefs about their experiences.
At its heart, it is about solidarity and social justice. It believes in the possibility for positive coping, whole-life recovery, and learning to listen to voices without torment and distress. No one is 'too ill' to benefit.

The HVN stance is one of respectful curiosity about the myriad ways people have of understanding voices, visions, sensory experiences and altered state of consciousness; it seeks to support people to make sense of their experiences, on their own terms. So despite the well-established link between hearing voices and traumatic and adverse life experiences, the HVN explicitly accepts all explanations for hearing voices which may include an array of belief systems, including spiritual, religious, paranormal, technological, cultural, counter-cultural, philosophical, medical, and so on. Research suggests that 'non-Western' cultures have something to teach us about how to live more peacefully with voices. For example, there is evidence that in the US, people are more likely to see their voices as a consequence of a brain disease, to use diagnostic labels and to report violent commands whereas in Ghana and India people reported rich relationships with their voices and insisted that their predominant or entire experience of the voices was positive (Luhrmann et al., 2015). The acceptance of a diversity of explanations for hearing voices has been crucial in developing the HVN internationally, without trying to export and impose Western ideas and assumptions about the mind or human experience.

Further reading

www.hearing-voices.org

www.intervoiceonline.org

References

Luhrmann, T.M., Padmavati, R., Tharoor, H. et al. (2015). Differences in voice-hearing experiences of people with psychosis in the USA, India and Ghana: Interview-based study. *British Journal of Psychiatry, 206,* 41–44.

Romme, M. & Escher, S. (Eds.) (1998). *Accepting voices* (2nd edn.). London: MIND Publications.

Romme, M. & Escher, S. (2000). *Making sense of voices: A guide for mental health professionals working with voice-hearers.* London: MIND Publications.

Romme, M., Escher, S., Dillon, J. et al. (Eds.) (2009). *Living with voices: 50 stories of recovery.* Ross-on-Wye: PCCS Books.

Appendix 12

Leeds Survivor Led Crisis Service

'I feel like talking to you all is replenishing the hope in my soul' (visitor feedback).

Leeds Survivor Led Crisis Service (LSLCS) was set up in 1999 by a group of mental health service users who campaigned to develop a place of sanctuary that was an alternative to a diagnostic, medical approach to mental health crisis. The organisation continues to be governed, managed and staffed by people with direct experience of mental health problems, some of whom are trained as counsellors or therapists

LSLCS provides an alternative to psychiatric hospitalisation, A&E, police custody and other statutory services, though offering the following:

- Dial House – crisis house offering sanctuary in a homely environment, one-to-one and peer support 6pm – 2am Monday, Wednesday and Friday-Sunday. Dial House @ Touchstone – Crisis service for people from Black and Minority Ethnic groups, 6–11pm Tuesday and Thursday.
- Connect Helpline – support and information by phone and online, 6pm-2am every night of the year.
- Group Work – includes Deaf mental health support group, LGBT group, Trans support group and Hearing Voices group.
- Leeds Suicide Bereavement Service (in partnership with Leeds Mind).
- Well Bean Crisis Café, 6pm–1am Saturday-Monday (Partnership with Touchstone).

Therapeutically, LSLCS is based on the Person Centred Approach, a phenomenological philosophy, which aspires to understand the world from the individual's perspective, rather than the label that they have been given. A central tenet of the Person Centred Approach is a belief in the tendency to acutalise – that people do the best they can, in the circumstances they are in, with the resources they have. Most of the work is with people at high risk of suicide and/or self-injury. In 2016, suicide was a presenting issue to Dial House in 65 per cent of visits, and self-injury in 49 per cent. Extensive support is also offered to survivors of trauma. During 2016, 65 per cent of visitors to Dial House had experienced sexual abuse in the past and/or in the present, rape or sexual violence.

The therapeutic approach of offering empathy, congruence and unconditional positive regard means that visitors with complex trauma issues are able to develop good relationships with workers, which often contrasts with their experiences within the psychiatric system. This non-judgemental, non-medical, validating approach leads to them feeling able to safely talk about their life histories and mental health issues. Building on this, the service has started to use the concept of 'formulation' to provide visitors a space to collaborate on composing a brief narrative – one which often links their current difficulties to trauma, abuse and neglect in their past – and which, when complete, will help them to understand themselves better and assist workers in other services to develop more therapeutic, trusting relationships with them.

This non-diagnostic alternative to the medical mainstream is very highly valued by visitors and callers – many of whom have been excluded from other services and/or have forensic histories and diagnoses such as 'personality disorder'. The approach to risk is to give people as much trust and control as possible, rather than being driven by a culture of fear and blame, in the knowledge that not all risky events can be prevented. Staff themselves are supported with regular supervision.

'It is different to other services – it is easier to talk to staff. Staff are nice. They don't judge you or put a label on you – saying "that's what's wrong with you."'

In defining itself in opposition to mainstream psychiatry, and locating itself firmly outside statutory provision, the service articulates its approach as survivor led, person centred and trauma informed. Evaluations have highlighted these five essential elements of effective support:

- Listening:
  'Sometimes it don't take a genius to work out that if you sit down and listen to someone and acknowledge the way they're feeling – that it's alright to feel shit – then they're gonna feel better.'

- Treating people with warmth, kindness and respect:
  'Just a short note to say thanks to Katharine for helping me to wash my hair. It seems like such a simple thing to help with, but it is the fact that Dial House are there to help with everything including simple things which makes Dial House such a unique and fantastic place.'

- Not feeling judged or assessed:
  'Can talk about absolutely anything and be validated, heard, accepted!'

- Being in a different and calm environment:
  'Thank you for getting me away from the funny farm for a couple of hours, the peace and quiet was a nice change from the noisy, hectic, crazy ward.'

- Peer support
  'It gives me a break. By being around people in the same situation as you, you are not having to feel ashamed.'

LSLCS is recognised as a centre of excellence and innovation, and has won national awards from *The Guardian*, Community Care, Charity Times, Investors in People, the Charity Evaluation Service and the Duke of York's Community Initiative. It has consistently demonstrated that it is possible to provide effective, compassionate and respectful alternatives to a diagnostic approach to distress, and similar projects have now been planned or set up in various places including London, Bristol and Hertfordshire.

Fiona Venner, Chief Executive of Leeds Survivor Led Crisis Service.

Further reading

http://www.lslcs.org.uk/

References

James, A. (2010). A beacon of hope. *Mental Health Today*, February, 18–19.
Venner, F. & Noad, M. (2013). Beacon of hope. In S. Coles, S. Keenan & B. Diamond (Eds.), *Madness contested: Power and practice* (pp.332–348). Ross-on-Wye: PCCS Books.

Appendix 13

Sharing Voices Bradford

Sharing Voices Bradford (SVB) is a community development mental health organisation established in 2002. It supports marginalised black and minority ethnic (BME) communities across the Bradford area to increase self-help/care, promote health and wellbeing, and recovery, and prevent mental distress. This includes diverse Central Eastern European, South Asian, African and African Caribbean peoples, along with asylum seekers/refugees and minority white and faith communities.

The aims of SVB are:

- Tackle stigma experienced by people living with mental distress.
- Provide information on mental health services.
- Promoting diversity.
- Breaking down barriers.
- Bringing diverse people and communities together.
- Provide an information and signposting service.
- Provide feedback to service providers to improve quality of mental health services.
- Stimulate debate on mental health and wellbeing.
- Partnership work with voluntary community sector, statutory service providers and local communities.

The project is based on the belief that an individual's mental health difficulties often arise from issues around poverty, racism, unemployment, loneliness, family conflicts and relationship difficulties, and cannot be understood simply in terms of biology. As such, the project does not use a diagnostic model of mental distress, but instead listens to people's own explanations and helps them find their own solutions to problems, while respecting and supporting their own belief systems. People with lived experiences of mental distress are at the centre of this work and shape its development, and 'choice' and 'participation' remain central so that people become active in developing their own pathways to recovery. The aim is to engage BME individuals and communities in an inclusive and progressive manner which values their cultural, religious, linguistic, and spiritual backgrounds.

Much of the project's work is done in partnership with service providers such as the Bradford District Care Trust (BDCT), GPs, and social workers. It also has partnerships with statutory primary and secondary services, schools, voluntary and faith organisations. SVB's Community Development Workers use methods derived from community development work to engage, support and develop the capacity of individuals in order to address issues around mental distress, isolation and promote social inclusion. SVB delivers and supports an extensive range of one-to-one befriending interventions, self-help/self-care groups, family outreach and community engagement across BME communities and other minority groups including specific projects with South Asian men, South Asian women, young BME people, older people from BME communities, Bangladeshi women, and many others. Refugees and asylum seekers are offered support, information and co-counselling.

The overall aim is to promote and enable the development of services that are aligned closely to the principles and objectives of 'Delivering Race Equality' (Department of Health, 2003) and the local Implementation Site, ensuring interventions are in line with the cultural and spiritual norms of local communities.

SVB's partnership work in schools, with inpatient wards and with an Imam employed by a local Muslim charity have been cited as examples of good practice (Care Services Improvement Partnership/NIMHE, 2008) for demonstrating the three principles of active participation of service user/carer; multi-disciplinary work; and strengths, resiliences and aspirations.

Ishtiaq Ahmed, Community Development Manager, Sharing Voices Bradford.

Further reading

http://sharingvoices.net/mentalhealth/about-us/

References

Care Services Improvement Partnership/NIMHE (2008). *Three keys to a shared approach in mental health.* London: Author.

Department of Health (2003). *Delivering race equality: A framework for action.* London: Author. Available from: http://www.thehealthwell.info/node/24349

Appendix 14

MAC-UK

MAC-UK is a London-based charity founded by a clinical psychologist and a group of excluded young people in 2008. MAC-UK works primarily with communities of excluded and vulnerable young people, including those in contact with the criminal justice system. Generational cycles of deprivation and exclusion borne from deep social inequalities mean that the young people are often from minority ethnic groups and experience poverty, racism, domestic violence, abuse, neglect and limited exposure to social mobility opportunities (Youth Justice Work Group, 2012). As a result many are excluded from school and are either homeless, in care or exploited from an early age and so are at high risk of entering an offending lifestyle. They are more likely to have poor mental health, learning difficulties and other complex needs. Equality of access to healthcare is the hallmark of a civilised society. However, evidence indicates that these most marginalised communities are being failed by our mainstream healthcare system and specifically by the structure of child and adolescent mental health services.

MAC-UK applies a whole systems, prevention and early intervention approach to mental health service transformation, made up of three key components: outreach; co-production; and psychologically informed services. We have a social, not medical, model of mental health, recognising that young people's mental health is not just what's in their heads, it's about what is in their worlds. We want it to be possible for every excluded young person to access and shape the services that are there to support them. This requires a radically different approach to the design and delivery of mental health provision.

MAC-UK staff and young people have developed the INTEGRATE approach, a framework for psychologically-informed services which recognises the multiple social impacts on young people (Zlotowitz et al., 2016). INTEGRATE draws on a range of psychological concepts, particularly Community Psychology, Attachment Theory, AMBIT (a mentalisation-based team working approach; see Bevington et al., 2012), Ecological Systems Theory and Narrative Therapy. For example, co-producing educational films can help young people to challenge the often dominant cultural narratives about 'gang members', 'hood rats', 'chavs' or 'young offenders' that they feel are imposed upon them, and to make different stories visible. One of the aims of INTEGRATE is to influence wider social change that addresses the social determinants of mental health and wellbeing, as well as promoting a wider understanding of young people's needs. Services based on this approach have run across London in partnership with local statutory agencies such as NHS Trusts and councils. Staff have been seconded in from these local agencies supporting the integrated nature of the services. Each has developed its own way of working in line with local needs and strengths.

There are several non-linear phases to the approach. They are:

PHASE 1 – Engagement

The building of trusted relationships with young people is essential. This is achieved by employing 'gatekeepers' (key trusted community members), adopting a peer-to-peer referral system, and staff 'hanging out' with young people. Peer influence attracts young people to the service and allows young people to trust staff more readily.

PHASE 2 – Youth-led activities

The approach emphasises the importance of 'doing with' not 'doing to' young people. The activities within a service are therefore fully co-produced with the young people and the process is considered as important as the outcome.

PHASE 3 – Streetherapy and psychologically-informed environments

We go to wherever the young people are, basing the work in the heart of the communities and providing flexible and responsive 'Streetherapy', in which staff engage in therapeutic conversations wherever and whenever the young person feels comfortable. Psychological methods such as weekly team formulating sessions are embedded in the structure to keep mental health and wellbeing at the heart of the projects.

PHASE 4 – Building bridges

Young people can ask for help with a range of needs, from housing support to benefits applications and finding employment. Staff draw on the project's wider partners and relationships, building bridges between resources, opportunities and the young people.

PHASE 5 – Championing change

Young people express their frustrations with their social worlds, and the team appreciates that community and social context factors contribute vastly to young people's mental health. Staff find ways to work in partnership with young people to create social change. Young people frequently join staff to train other agencies on the impact of health and social inequalities on their lives.

Impact and evaluation

MAC-UK has been successful in engaging groups of young people who are traditionally seen as 'hard to reach', marginalised, and involved in offending or at risk of offending.

> 'They came here and not judged no one, they don't ask your history, or what you look like, or how you dress, they came with open arms and gave you a fresh start. They put people first and they always stand for us, even though we cause headaches.'

> '... it really makes a difference... I was sure I was going down [to prison] but [the INTEGRATE worker] got up there and said about me and told them what about my goals and what I was trying to do... and he [the judge] actually praised me for trying to change...'

Approximately one-third of young people in evaluation samples reported a level of wellbeing that would warrant referral to a mental health service. Over time a non-pathologising narrative of mental health increased and stigma around it reduced.

'… it would just freak me out [the topic of mental health] … I'd run a mile.. But I now know lots of people can get stressed out… it's about doing positive things so you have good mental health…'

MAC-UK is independently evaluated by the Centre for Mental Health, and this research is ongoing. The charity also carries out internal audits and evaluation. As it works at multiple levels and across various domains, a wide variety of areas of impact have been noted including employment, education, offending, policy influence and change in NHS practice. Further details can be found on the MAC-UK website or in the Centre for Mental Health briefing paper (Durcan et al., 2017). It has won many awards, including the Times Charity of the Year 2011 and Positive Practice in Mental Health Criminal Justice Award 2014.

We want all providers to adopt the approach into their core fabric of their governance, culture and practice. It's time for a bold new era of co-produced services and psychologically-informed environments being made available in the places that excluded communities can reach and through people that they trust.

Liz Greenaway (Trainee Clinical Psychologist) **Jade Templer** (Trainee Clinical Psychologist) **Grace Clayton** (Honorary Assistant) **Dr Laura Casale** (Clinical Community Psychologist and Clinical Lead, Projects) **Dr Sally Zlotowitz** (Clinical Community Psychologist and Clinical Lead, Dissemination).

Further reading

http://www.mac-uk.org/about-us/

References

Bevington, D., Fuggle, P., Fonagy, P. et al. (2012). Adolescent Mentalization-Based Integrative Therapy (AMBIT): A new integrated approach to working with the most hard to reach adolescents with severe complex mental health needs. *Child and Adolescent Mental Health, 18,* 46–51.

Durcan, G., Zlotowitz, S. & Stubbs, J. (2017). *Meeting us where we're at: Learning from Integrate's work with excluded young people. Briefing paper.* Centre for Mental Health. Available at: www.centreformentalhealth.org.uk/meeting-us-where-were-at

Youth Justice Working Group (2012). *Rules of engagement: Changing the heart of youth justice* [online] Available from: www.centreforsocialjustice.org.uk/library/rules-engagement-changing-heart-youth-justice

Zlotowitz, S., Barker, C., Moloney, O. & Howard, C. (2016). Service users as the key to service change? The development of an innovative intervention for excluded young people. *Child and Adolescent Mental Health, 21,* 102–108.

References

Andersen, T. (Ed.) (1991). *The reflecting team: Dialogues and dialogues about the dialogues.* London: Norton.

American Psychiatric Association (2013). *Diagnostic and statistical manual of mental disorders* (5th edn. *DSM-5*). Washington, DC: Author.

Arthur, E., Seymour, A., Dartnall, M. et al. (2013). *Trauma-informed practice guide.* British Colombia Centre of Excellence for Women's Health. Available from: http://bccewh.bc.ca/wp-content/uploads/2012/05/2013_TIP-Guide.pdf

Barker, P. & Buchanan-Barker, P. (2005). *The Tidal Model: A guide for mental health professionals.* London, New York: Brunner-Routledge.

Blue Knot Foundation (2012). *Practice guidelines for treatment of complex trauma and trauma informed care and service delivery.* Author. Available from: http://www.blueknot.org.au/ABOUT-US/Our-Documents/Publications/Practice-Guidelines

Bracken, P. (2002). *Trauma: Culture, meaning and philosophy.* Chichester: John Wiley & Sons.

Burstow, B. (2003). Toward a radical understanding of trauma and trauma work. *Violence against Women, 9*(11), 1293–1317.

Burton, M. & Kagan, C. (2011). Towards a really social psychology: Liberation psychology beyond Latin America. In M. Montero & C.C. Sonn (Eds.), *The psychology of liberation: Theory and applications* (pp.53–72). New York: Springer.

Butler, G. (1998). Clinical formulation. In A.S. Bellack & M. Hersen (Eds.), *Comprehensive clinical psychology* (pp.1–23). Oxford: Pergamon.

Cassidy, J. & Shaver, P.R. (Eds.) (2008). *Handbook of attachment: Theory, research and clinical applications.* New York, London: Guilford Press.

Clayton, S. & Hughes, G. (2016). The use of film and creative media to liberate young refugees and asylum-seeking people from disempowering identities: A dialogical approach. In T. Afuape & G. Hughes (Eds.), *Liberation practices: Towards emotional wellbeing through dialogue* (pp.89–99). London, New York: Routledge.

Clements, J. (2005). *People with autism behaving badly: Helping people with ASD move on from behavioural and emotional challenges.* London: Jessica Kingsley Publishers.

Clemon, O. (2016). 'Holdin' on': Using music technology as a tool of cultural liberation with respect to performing masculinities at a young offenders' institution. In T. Afuape & G. Hughes, G. (Eds.), *Liberation practices: Towards emotional wellbeing through dialogue* (pp.51–63). London, New York: Routledge.

Coleman, R. (2017). *The Ron Coleman story.* http://www.workingtorecovery.co.uk/ron-coleman/the-ron-coleman-story.aspx

Corrie, S. & Lane, D. (2010). *Constructing stories, telling tales: A guide to formulation in applied psychology.* London: Karnac.

Courtois, C. & Ford, J. (2013). *Treatment of complex trauma: A sequenced, relationship-based approach.* New York: Guilford Press.

Craddock, N. & Mynors-Wallis, L. (2014). Psychiatric diagnosis: Impersonal, imperfect and important. The *British Journal of Psychiatry, 204*(2), 93–95.

Crittenden, P.M. (2002). Attachment, information processing, and psychiatric disorder. *World Psychiatry, 1*(2), 72–75.

Crittenden, P.M. (2005). Attachment theory, psychopathology, and psychotherapy: The Dynamic-Maturational Approach. *Psicoterapia, 30,* 171–182.

Crittenden, P.M. (2006). A dynamic-maturational model of attachment. *Australian Association of Family Therapy Volume, 27*(2), 105–115.

Crittenden, P.M. & Dallos, R. (2009). All in the family: Integrating attachment and family systems theories. *Clinical Child Psychology and Psychiatry, 14,* 389–409.

Cromby, J., Harper, D. & Reavey, P. (2013). *Psychology, mental health and distress.* Basingstoke: Palgrave Macmillan.

Dallos, R. & Stedmon, J. (2014). Systemic formulation: Mapping the family dance. In L. Johnstone & R. Dallos (Eds.), *Formulation in psychology and psychotherapy: Making sense of people's problems* (pp.67–95). London: Routledge.

Davar, B. (2016). Alternatives or a way of life? In J. Russo & A. Sweeney (Eds.), *Searching for a rose garden: Challenging psychiatry, fostering mad studies* (pp.14–19). Monmouth: PCCS Books.

Denborough, D. (2008). *Collective narrative practice: Responding to individuals, groups and communities who have experienced trauma.* Adelaide: Dulwich.

Dillon, J. & May, R. (2003). Reclaiming experience. *Openmind, 120,* 16–17.

Division of Clinical Psychology (2011). *Good practice guidelines on the use of psychological formulation.* Leicester: British Psychological Society.

Engle, R.L. & Davis, B.J. (1963). Medical diagnosis: Present, past, and future I. Present concepts of the meaning and limitations of medical diagnosis. *Archives of Internal Medicine, 112,* 108–115.

Freyd, J.J. & Birrell, P.J. (2013). *Blind to betrayal.* Hoboken, NJ: John Wiley & Sons.

Fricker, M. (2007). *Epistemic injustice: Power and the ethics of knowing.* Oxford: Oxford University Press.

Frosh, S. (2007). Disintegrating qualitative research. *Theory & Psychology, 17*(5), 635–653.

Gilbert, P. (2007). *Psychotherapy for counselling and depression* (3rd edn.). London: Sage.

Goldstein, K. (1995). *The organism: A holistic approach to biology.* New York: Zone Books.

Grandin, T. (1984). My experiences as an autistic child and review of selected literature. *Journal of Orthomolecular Psychiatry, 13,* 144–174.

Grant, A. (2015). Demedicalising misery: Welcoming the human paradigm in mental health nurse education. *Nurse Education Today, 35,* 50–53.

Grant, A., Leigh-Pippard, H. & Short, N.P. (2015). Re-storying narrative identity: A dialogical study of mental health recovery and survival. *Journal of Psychiatric and Mental Health Nursing, 22,* 278–286.

Greenhalgh, T. & Hurwitz, M. (1999). Narrative based medicine: Why study narratives? *British Medical Journal, 318,* 48–50.

Haack, S. (1996). *Deviant logic, fuzzy logic: Beyond the formalism.* Chicago: The University of Chicago Press.

Hagan, T. & Gregory, K. (2001). Groupwork with survivors of childhood sexual abuse. In P. Pollock (Ed.), *Cognitive analytic therapy for adult survivors of sexual abuse* (pp.190–205). Chichester: Wiley.

Hagan, T. & Smail, D. (1997a). Power-mapping 1. Background and basic methodology. *Journal of Community and Applied Social Psychology, 7,* 257–267.

Hagan, T. & Smail, D. (1997b). Power-mapping II. Practical application: The example of child sexual abuse. *Journal of Community and Applied Social Psychology, 7,* 269–284.

Harper, D. & Moss, D. (2003). A different kind of chemistry? Reformulating 'formulation'. *Clinical Psychology, 25,* 6–10.

Harper, D. & Spellman, D. (2013). Formulation and narrative therapy: Telling a different story. In L. Johnstone & R. Dallos (Eds.), *Formulation in psychology and psychotherapy: Making sense of people's problems* (2nd edn.), pp.96–120. London, New York: Routledge.

Hawtin, S. & Moore, J. (1998). Empowerment or collusion? The social context of person- centred therapy. In E. Lambers & B. Thorne (Eds.), *Person-centred therapy: A European perspective.* London: Sage.

Herman, J.L. (2001). *Trauma and recovery: The aftermath of violence - from domestic abuse to political terror.* New York: Basic Books.

Jankovic, J., Bremner, S., Bogie, M. et al. (2012). Trauma and suicidality in war affected communities. *European Psychiatry, 28,* 514–520.

Jetten, J., Haslam, C. & Haslam, S.A. (Eds.) (2012). *The social cure: Identity, health and well-being.* New York and Hove: Psychology Press.

Johnstone, L. (2013). Controversies and debates about formulation. In L. Johnstone, L. & R. Dallos (Eds.) *Formulation in psychology and psychotherapy: Making sense of people's problems* (2nd edn.), pp.260–289. London, New York: Routledge.

Kerr, L.K. (2014). Can DSM diagnoses be other than pejorative? Global Summit on Diagnostic Alternatives. Available from: http://dxsummit.org/archives/2014

Kuyken, W. (2006). Evidence-based case formulation: Is the emperor clothed? In N. Tarrier (Ed.) *Case formulation in cognitive behaviour therapy: The treatment of challenging and complex cases,* pp.12–35. London, New York: Routledge.

LeDoux, J. E. (1999). *The emotional brain.* London: Phoenix.

Lee, D. & James, S. (2012). *The compassionate mind approach to recovery from trauma.* London: Robinson.

Leeming, D., Boyle, M. & MacDonald, J. (2009). Accounting for psychological problems: How user-friendly are psychosocial formulations? *Clinical Psychology Forum, 200,* 12–17.

LeFrancois, B.A. (2016). Foreword. In J. Russo & A. Sweeney (Eds.), *Searching for a rose garden: Challenging psychiatry, fostering mad studies* (pp.v–vii.) Monmouth: PCCS Books.

Longden, E. (2013). *Learning from the voices in my head* (TED Books, Book 39). TED Conferences.

Maercker, A., Brewin, C.R., Bryant, R.A. et al. (2013). Diagnosis and classification of disorders specifically associated with stress: Proposals for *ICD-11. World Psychiatry, 12*(3), I98–206.

McClelland, L. (2014). Reformulating the impact of social inequalities. In L. Johnstone & R. Dallos (Eds.), *Formulation in psychology and psychotherapy: Making sense of people's problems* (pp.121–144.) London, New York: Routledge.

McInnis, E.E. (2017). Black psychology: A paradigm for a less oppressive clinical psychology? *Clinical Psychology Forum, 299,* 3–8.

Mead, S. & Filson, B. (2016). Becoming part of each other's narratives: Intentional Peer Support. In J. Russo & A. Sweeney (Eds.), *Searching for a rose garden: Challenging psychiatry, fostering mad studies* (pp.109–117.) Monmouth: PCCS Books.

Meichenbaum, D. (1993). Changing conceptions of cognitive behavior modification: Retrospect and prospect. *Journal of Consulting and Clinical Psychology, 61*(2), 202–204.

Ncube-Millo, N. & Denborough, D. (2007). *Tree of life – mainstreaming psychosocial care and support: A manual for facilitators.* Randburg: REPSSI.

Nelson, G. & Prilleltensky, I. (2010). *Community psychology: In pursuit of liberation and well-being.* Basingstoke: Palgrave Macmillan.

Orford, J. (2008). *Community psychology: Challenges, controversies and emerging consensus.* Chichester: Wiley.

Otto, H. & Keller, H. (2014). *Different faces of attachment: Cultural variations on a universal theme.* Cambridge: Cambridge University Press.

Panksepp, J. (1998). *Affective neuroscience.* Oxford: Oxford University Press.

Pinderhughes, H., Davis R. & Williams M. (2015). *Adverse community experiences and resilience: A framework for addressing and preventing community trauma.* Oakland, CA: Prevention Institute.

Redhead, S., Johnstone, L. & Nightingale, J. (2015). Clients' experiences of formulation in cognitive behaviour therapy. *Psychology and Psychotherapy: Theory, Research and Practice, 88*(4), 453–467.

Romme. M. & Escher, S. (2000). *Making sense of voices: A guide for mental health professionals.* London: Mind Publications.

Romme, M., Escher, S., Dillon, J. et al. (2009). *Living with voices: 50 stories of recovery.* Ross on Wye: PCCS Books.

Rosenberg, C.E. (2002). *The tyranny of diagnosis: Specific entities and individual experience.* The Milbank Quarterly, 80, 237–260.

Rosen, C., Jones, N., Longden, E. et al. (2017). Exploring the intersections of trauma, structural adversity, and psychosis among a primarily African-American sample: A mixed-methods analysis. *Frontier Psychiatry 8*(57). doi:10.3389/fpsyt.2017.00057

Russo, J. (2016). Towards our own framework, or reclaiming madness, Part two. In J. Russo & A. Sweeney (Eds.), *Searching for a rose garden: Challenging psychiatry, fostering mad studies* (pp.59–68.) Monmouth: PCCS Books.

Sackett, D. (2002). *Evidence-based medicine: How to practise and teach evidence-based medicine* (2nd edn.). London: Churchill Livingstone.

Schafer, R. (1980). Narration in the psychoanalytic dialogue. *Critical Inquiry, 7*(1), 29–53.

Schon D.A. (1987). *Educating the reflective practitioner.* San Francisco: Jossey-Bass.

Seikkula, J. & Arnkil, T.E. (2006). *Dialogical meetings in social networks.* London: Karnac.

Shevlin, M., McAnee, G., Bentall, R. & Murphy, J. (2015). Specificity of association between adversities and the occurrence and co-occurrence of paranoia and hallucinations: Evaluating the stability of childhood risk in an adverse adult environment. *Psychosis, 7*(3), 206–216.

Skills for Health, Health Education England and Skills for Care (2016). *Mental Health Core Skills Education and Training Framework.* Bristol: Author.

Skultans, V. (2003). From damaged nerves to masked depression: Inevitability and hope in Latvian psychiatric narratives. *Social Science and Medicine, 56*(12), 2421–2431.

Somasundaram, D. & Sivayokan, S. (2013). Rebuilding community resilience in a post-war context: Developing insight and recommendations – a qualitative study in Northern Sri Lanka. *International Journal of Mental Health Systems, 7*(3). doi:10.1186/1752-4458-7-3

Speed, B. (1999). Individuals in context and contexts in individuals. *Australian and New Zealand Journal of Family Therapy, 20*, 131–138.

Spence, D.P. (1982). *Narrative truth and historical truth: Meaning and interpretation in psychoanalysis.* London: Norton.

Steel, Z., Chey, T., Silove, D. et al. (2009). Association of torture and other potentially traumatic events with mental health outcomes among populations exposed to mass conflict and displacement: A systematic review and meta-analysis. *Journal of the American Medical Association, 302*(5), 537–549.

Sweeney, S., Clement, S., Filson, B. & Kennedy, A. (2016). Trauma-informed mental healthcare in the UK: What is it and how can we further its development? *Mental Health Review Journal, 21*(3), 174–192.

Thomas, P. & Longden, E. (2013). Madness, childhood adversity and narrative psychiatry: Caring and the moral imagination. *Medical Humanities, 39*(2), 119–125.

Ulster University (2015). *Towards a better future: The trans-generational impact of the Troubles on mental health. Commission for Victims and Survivors.* Ulster: Author. Available from: http://www.cvsni.org/images/policyresearch/pubs/march_2015/Towards_a_Bette_Future_for_Web.pdf

United Nations Human Rights Commission (2017). *Report of the Special Rapporteur on the right of everyone to the enjoyment of the highest attainable standard of physical and mental health.* New York: United Nations General Assembly.

van der Kolk, B. (2014). *The body keeps the score: Brain, mind, and body in the healing of trauma.* New York: Viking.

Waddingham, R. (2013). *Symptom or experience: Does language matter?* Available from: www.madinamerica.com/2013/08/does-language-matter

White, M. (2000). Reflecting teamwork as definitional ceremony revisited. In M. White (Ed.), *Reflections on narrative practice: Essays and Interviews* (pp.59–88.) Adelaide: Dulwich Centre Publications.

Wylie, M. S. (2010). The long shadow of trauma: Childhood abuse may be our number one public health issue. *Psychotherapy Networker, March/April.* Available from: https://www.psychotherapynetworker.org/magazine/article/417/the-long-shadow-of-trauma

Printed in the USA
CPSIA information can be obtained
at www.ICGtesting.com
LVHW072056211123
764440LV00012B/368